Ghostly PLACES

A collection of chilling stories about haunted places from the newspapers of Tennessee

Brought to you by the 125 newspapers who make up
Tennessee Press Association and Tennessee Press Service

TENNESSEE
PRESS
ASSOCIATION

TPS
TENNESSEE PRESS SERVICE

Ghostly Places

A collection of chilling stories about haunted places
from the newspapers of Tennessee

©2017 Tennessee Press Service
books@tnpress.com
412 N. Cedar Bluff Rd, Suite 403
Knoxville, Tennessee 37923

ISBN13: 978-0-9987546-4-2

Printed and Bound in the United States of America

Editor: Kevin Slimp
Design & Cover Illustration ©2017 by Kevin Slimp

"For who can wonder that man should feel
a vague belief in tales of disembodied spirits
wandering through those places which they
once dearly affected, when he himself, scarcely
less separated from his old world than they, is
for ever lingering upon past emotions
and bygone times, and hovering, the ghost
of his former self, about the places and people
that warmed his heart of old?"

Charles Dickens

Ghostly PLACES

Table of Contents

Introduction 1

Mrs. Haynes Found Dead! 3

Was It Suicide or Murder? 9

The Shadow People and a Suspicious Death 15

Haunted Knoxville Ghost Tours 26

Knock, Knock. Nobody's There 27

Most Haunted Places in McNairy County 31

The Thomas House 35

The Bell Witch 39

The Haunting of Sensabaugh Tunnel 43

Captain Clay's Black Horse 47

A Soldier's Experience in the Tennessee Mountains 51

Finding Spirits in Greeneville 59

Tales of the Gravedigger: Part 1 67

Tales of the Gravedigger: Part 2 79

The Spiritual Realm 89

The Downtown Prankster of Rogersville 95

Blount County Ghost Busters 99

Is There a Ghost in the Westwood House? 104

The Blue Hole 105

Just Outside Knoxville: Murder in Dr. Baker's House 109

The Ghost Upstairs 113

A Spirit Lives On at Greene's Antiques 117

Ghostly Places Crossword Puzzle 123

INTRODUCTION

When the decision was made to publish a series of books based on stories in Tennessee newspapers, most of us thought we would be inundated with stories about high school sports champions and heros across the state. Imagine my surprise when we began to receive stories about haunted places from every corner of the Volunteer State.

It seems that just about everyone is fascinated with the idea of haunted places. You may have been on one of the many ghost tours around the state, or you may have experienced a paranormal event of your own.

Whatever the case, we hope you enjoy reading these stories about haunted place and those who seek to encounter them so they can teach us more about them.

Special thanks goes to my friend David S. Wells, general manager, Tennessee Press, for the original idea to publish this book and for his editing assistance. I would also like to thank J. Adam Smith, Haunted Knoxville Ghost Tours, for his help uncovering some of the stories which took place around Knoxville.

Thanks also goes to authors Ashley Hagan and J.J. White for their editing assistance with this project.

Oh, and allow me to share one piece of advice: Read these stories in a well lit room. You don't want to be alone in the dark while reading *Ghostly Places*.

Thank you for joining us on this adventure.

Kevin Slimp

CHAPTER ONE

Mrs. Haynes Found
DEAD!

Widow of Shoe Wholesaler Believed Suicide; Sustained Stab in Neck

Knoxville News Sentinel
From April 19, 1928 Issue

Mrs. Lillian Haynes, 52, widow of W. P. Haynes, formerly of the Haynes-Henson Shoe Co. and mother of W.P. Haynes Jr. and the late J.P. Haynes, is dead from a stab wound in the neck.

She was found at 11:45 last night, lying on the floor in her locked and darkened bedroom at 2310 N. Broadway, by her son, William P. A butcher knife was nearby.

Coroner John Scott and Harry Burke, chief of the Police Homicide Bureau, said today they were practically positive Mrs. Haynes committed suicide. If so, it is

MORE ABOUT
Mrs. Haynes'
Death
STARTS ON PAGE ONE

screen apparently undisturbed.

Switching on the lights, he found the body, fully dressed.

Fearing that she had been murdered, he called police. On the arrival of Burke and Police Captain Montgomery, Coroner Scott was called. No evidence of robbery or disturbance in the room was found, the officers reported.

A writing desk near the body and other probable places were searched for a farewell communication, but none was found the coroner said.

"Death may have resulted two hours before the body was found," the coroner said.

Altho preparing for inquest by coroner's jury, Coroner Scott said that all indications were that death was self inflicted.

In House Alone.

Both Mrs. J. P. Haynes and William, Jr., were absent and, as far as is known no other person was in the house at Mrs. Haynes' death.

"Investigation of the house revealed nothing missing or disarranged," Mr. Burke said. "We found nothing that pointed to anything but suicide."

Mrs. Haynes had been a member of the old Broad Street Methodist

Knoxville News Sentinel
April 19, 1928

3

Knoxville's twelfth suicide this year and the first woman to kill herself.

Police had not given up investigation today, Mike Cross, criminal identification expert, was to try to take fingerprints in the bedroom this afternoon.

Believe Grief Cause

Grief over the death of her younger son, J.P. Haynes, last year, was believed to be the cause of Mrs. Haynes' act, granting that she committed suicide.

"J.P.'s death took all the light out of her life," Mrs. James C. Renfro, 103 E. Fourth Ave, Mrs. Haynes' mother, said today.

"Yesterday she had some of his things out looking at them, a thing that always made her particularly despondent. Yet she seemed normal when she talked with me over the telephone for some time yesterday afternoon."

W.P. Haynes said today that although he was not positively convinced, he inclined to the opinion that his mother died by her own hand.

MRS. LILLIE HAYNES COMMITS SUICIDE

Widow Of Founder Of Large Wholesale Shoe Co., Found Dead By Son.

USED LARGE KNIFE

For Years Active In Religious, Charitable Work; Parents And Son Survive.

Mrs. Lillian Mae Renfroe Haynes, 52, widow of W. P. Haynes, wealthy wholesale shoe dealer, committed suicide last night by cutting her throat with a kitchen knife in her luxuriously furnished home, 2310 North Broadway.

Mrs. Haynes was found dead in her room on the second floor of the home about 11:45 o'clock when her son, William J. Haynes, Jr., returned home. On his arrival he called to his mother to inform her that he was at home. When no response came, the young man became alarmed and tried to open the door to her bed room. Finding the room locked from

Knoxville Journal
April 19, 1928

No Financial Worry

"She had no financial problems to bother her," he said, "but

4

WHERE MRS. HAYNES DIED

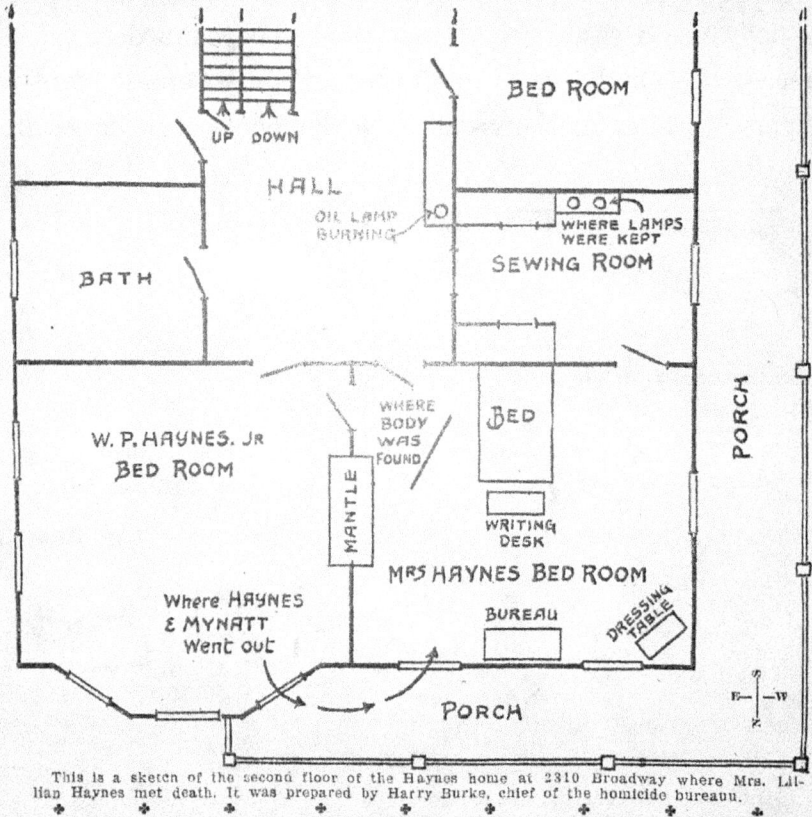

BED ROOM

HALL

UP DOWN

OIL LAMP
BURNING

WHERE LAMPS
WERE KEPT

SEWING ROOM

BATH

WHERE
BODY
WAS
FOUND

BED

W. P. HAYNES. JR
BED ROOM

MANTLE

WRITING
DESK

MRS HAYNES BED ROOM

Where HAYNES
& MYNATT
Went out

BUREAU

DRESSING
TABLE

PORCH

PORCH

This is a sketch of the second floor of the Haynes home at 2310 Broadway where Mrs. Lillian Haynes met death. It was prepared by Harry Burke, chief of the homicide bureau.

she had been despondent ever since my brother's death. She had also never fully got over my father's death."

Last night on entering the house, the son called to his mother and asked if Mrs. J.P. Haynes, the other son's widow was at home.

Getting no answer, he ran up the stairs and knocked on his mother's door. When the knocking drew no response, he became alarmed and went for his cousin, E.F. Mynatt, who lives next door.

5

They then called Mrs. Renfro. "I told Billy to go around and through the window." Mrs. Renfro said. When he reached the roof, the son found the window of his mother's room open, but the screen apparently undisturbed. Switching on the lights, he found the body fully dressed. Fearing that she had been murdered, he called police. On the arrival of Burke and Police Captain Montgomery, Coroner Scott was called. No evidence of robbery or dis-

PORCH

nd floor of the Haynes home at 2310 Broadway where Mrs. Lil-
s prepared by Harry Burke, chief of the homicide bureauu.

   ❖   ❖   ❖   ❖   ❖   ❖

which sets near the foot of her bed was a bit of yellow wrapping paper. It is a paper not more than eight inches square. The writing on it—Mrs. Haynes' handwriting—would furnish interesting speculation for a fiction detective.

The writing is two attempts at the solution of a News-Sentinel Letter Golf puzzle. It is that puzzle, published recently, which goes from PLANT to CROPS.

A rug now covers the only signs of Mrs. Haynes' death. The rug, running by the bed, cover two blood stains in the carpet beneath. One stain is about six or seven inches in diameter. The other is smaller.

Body Away From Stains

The body of Mrs. Haynes, however, was lying two or three feet from the farthest of these stains. Her head was lying on the corner of the hearth. For nearly the entire length of the wooden facing of the hearth some fluid had been spilled, the relatives said. They thought it was carbolic acid—fiery liquid like that which burned the victim's face, neck and one eye.

A small bottle, less than one-half filled with carbolic acid, was found on the end of the mantel nearest the body. The metal cover was lying in the floor. The label had been taken from the bottle.

The somberness of death still lingers in the house. Relatives and friends move about noiselessly. Here and there small groups of them converse in undertones.

Not an activity that would spark a suicide.

(Picture Album, momentos from Husband would ▭ sparking)

The notes are from famed Knoxville paranormal historian, J. Adam Smith, taken while researching the story of Mrs. Haynes death.

turbance in the room was found, the officers reported. A writing desk near the body and other probable places were searched for a farewell communication, but none was found, the coroner said. Altho preparing for inquest by coroner's jury, Coroner Scott said that all indications were that death was self inflicted.

In House Alone

Both Mrs. J. P. Haynes and William, Jr. were absent and, as far as is known, no other person was in the house at Mrs. Haynes death. "Investigation of the house revealed nothing missing or disarranged." Mr. Burke said. "We found nothing that pointed to anything but suicide." Mrs. Haynes had been a member of the old Broad Street Methodist Church, now consolidated with the Centenary Church, since childhood, her mother said. She was actively interested in charity as well as church work and was a founder of the Mount Rest Home, holding office as a director for years. She was secretary-treasurer of the Knox County Humane Society. "She had telephoned me yesterday regarding the purchase of a truck for Humane society work which we were to go and see about today." Mrs. Renfro said. Although funeral arrangements are not completed, services will be conducted at the Central M. E. Church, of which Mrs. Haynes was a member. Burial probably will not take place before Saturday.

Born Here

Mrs. Haynes was born in Knoxville on February 14, 1877, and has lived here all her life. She married William P. Haynes on February 24, 1897, and they lived for many years in the large Haynes home place on North Broadway.

Mrs. Haynes is survived by one son, W. P. Jr.; her parents Mr. and Mrs. J. C. Renfro, 103 E. Fourth-av; and one sister, Mrs. W.

W. Morrell, wife of the Rev. Morrell of Abingdon, Va.

Mrs. Haynes' husband, the late W. P. Haynes, was for years in the wholesale shoe business which his father, also named W. P. Haynes, founded. Her husband had been ill in health for a long time before his death last year.

MRS. LILLIE HAYNES COMMITTS SUICIDE

(Continued from Page One.)

vestigation was in progress at an early hour this morning

Mrs. Haynes was alone at home at the time she died. A pet bull dog was in the home and when the investigators arrived the dog did not show signs of having been disturbed by an intruder in the room as a relative had suggested as being probable.

Those entering the handsomely furnished home found the reception room, hall and dining room in perfect condition and nothing had been disarranged. It is believed that Mrs. Haynes suddenly decided to end her life after going from the sitting room to her bed room for the night.

Relatives said last night that Mrs. Haynes had been despondent at times since her son J. P. Haynes died. Her mother said the passing of her son took the sunshine from her home and made her feel despondent.

Mrs. Haynes was one of Knoxville's best know and greatly beloved women, a member of one of the city's oldest families, being the daughter of James C. and Laura Renfro, 193 East Fourth avenue.

She was a life long member of the

Knoxville Journal
April 19, 1928

CHAPTER TWO

Was It Suicide or
Was It Murder?

Haynes Case is 30-Year Mystery

By Lee Winfrey
Knoxville News Sentinel
From April 26, 1959 Issue

At 8:40 that night, said the cook Mamie Siler, the lights in the big Haynes home were switched off. Twenty minutes later they were back on.

In the dark interval Mrs. W. P. Haynes died, the victim of a knife thrust in her throat and searing carbolic acid forced into her mouth.

With her death a $108,000 estate changed hands. Two opulent diamond rings disappeared. And her home, a rambling two-story Broadway Landmark, was sentenced to destruction.

Mrs. Haynes, 52, owned much of the Haynes-Henson Shoe Co.,

9

founded in Knoxville in 1970 by her father-in-law. She lived at 2310 Broadway with her son, her daughter-in-law, and a vigilant bulldog named Jack.

The night she died only Jack was there, lying in the downstairs reception room with a bone the cook had given him.

Body Found By Son

Mrs. Haynes died in her bedroom upstairs, her head on a tiled hearth, her face, neck, and one eye seared with acid, a bloody discarded paring knife lying nearby.

Her son found the body, near midnight April 18, 1928.

The son, William P. Haynes, said he left home that night about 7:15. He had a date, he said, went to a movie at the Riviera, and got back home about 11:45.

The house was quiet, Jack the bulldog lay placidly downstairs. Mrs. Haynes' widowed daughter-in-law, Mrs. J. P. Haynes, had left the house several hours earlier to spend the night with a neighbor.

"I called upstairs to my mother." William P. Haynes told police later. "She didn't answer. I went upstairs and found her door locked. I got suspicious."

Young Haynes went next door and got his cousin, E. F. Mynatt. He called Mrs. James C. Renfro, Mrs. Haynes' mother, and she came back to the big quiet house with the two young men.

"Go around and go through the window, Billy." Mrs. Renfro told William P. Haynes.

Entered Bedroom Window

Young Haynes' bedroom was beside his mother's on the east side of the house. A second-story porch led past the win-

10

Was It Suicide or Was It Murder?
Haynes Case Is 30-Year Mystery

By LEE WINFREY

At 8:40 that night, said the cook Mamie Siler, the lights in the big Haynes home were switched off.

Twenty minutes later they were back on.

In the dark interval Mrs. W. P. Haynes died, the victim of a knife thrust in her throat and searing carbolic acid forced into her mouth.

With her death a $108,000 estate changed hands. Two opulent diamond rings disappeared. And her home, a rambling, two-story Broadway landmark, was sentenced to destruction.

Mrs. Haynes, 52, owned much of the Haynes-Henson Shoe Co., founded in Knoxville in 1870 by her father-in-law. She lived at 2310 Broadway with her son, her daughter-in-law, and a vigilant bulldog named Jack.

The night she died only Jack was there, lying in the downstairs reception room with a bone the cook had given him.

BODY FOUND BY SON

Mrs. Haynes died in her bedroom upstairs, her head on a tiled hearth, her face, neck, and one eye seared with acid, a bloody discarded paring knife lying nearby.

Her son found the body, near midnight April 18, 1929.

The son, William P. Haynes, said he left home that night about 7:15. He had a date, he said, went to a movie at the Riviera, and got back home about 11:45.

The house was quiet. Jack the bulldog lay placidly downstairs. Mrs. Haynes' widowed daughter-in-law, Mrs. J. P. Haynes, had left the house several hours earlier to spend the night with a neighbor.

"I called upstairs to my mother," William P. Haynes told police later. "She didn't answer. I went upstairs and found her door locked. I got suspicious."

Young Haynes went next door and got his cousin, E. F. Mynatt. He called Mrs. James C. Renfro, Mrs. Haynes' mother, and she came back to the big quiet house with the two young men.

"Go around and go through the window, Billy," Mrs. Renfro told William P. Haynes.

ENTERED BEDROOM WINDOW

Young Haynes' bedroom was beside his mother's on the east side of the house. A second-story porch led past the windows of both rooms. Accompanied by his cousin, young Haynes climbed out his bedroom window and stepped quickly down the porch to the window of his mother's room. It was unlocked, and they went in.

"Mynatt turned on the lights," said William P. Haynes. "She was dead. There were two pools of blood and a stained knife beside her. A one ounce bottle of carbolic acid, two thirds empty, stood on the mantel. We called the police."

The police,—Homicide Chief Harry Burke and Capt. John Montgomery, arrived and started up the stairs with young Haynes and Mynatt. Mynatt had a shotgun. It went off accidentally and blew a hole in the floor. Burke and Montgomery, perhaps unnerved by the blast, made a quick inspection of the bedroom and the body.

They emerged and called the death a suicide.

Mrs. Renfro's comment on their work was pungent. "The most bungling piece of work," she said, "that I have ever seen."

Next day a coroner's jury agreed with Mrs. Renfro. Mrs. Haynes, said the jury, "came to her death by foul means—at the hands of an unknown person."

COOK'S BOY-FRIEND QUIZZED

Shifting their verdict nimbly from suicide to murder, the police went to work. They quizzed the cook.

She'd been out back in her own little house, said the cook, and noted nothing but the on-and-off twinkling of the lights.

They grilled Sloan McNabb, a friend of the cook's who said at first he'd dated the cook and then gone home. Finally he admitted spending the night with the cook. But he hadn't been in the house where Mrs. Haynes had locked herself in with the bulldog Jack.

They questioned Ed Fernand, a young civil engineer and a friend of William P. Haynes. Fernand owned a small car similar to one seen near the house by a passing streetcar rider.

But Fernand was clean.

Two weeks went by without a solid suspect. Investigative minds began to think again of suicide. In an effort to clear the air, William P. Haynes brought down a Philadelphia detective, Peter Shelier, to make a new investigation.

Shelier took a two-day look-see and pronounced Mrs. Haynes a suicide.

The sheriff agreed with him. The city safety director didn't. And who felt the full force of their quandary?

The bulldog Jack.

WATCHDOG PASSES TEST

Jack, said all who knew him, was the model watchdog: Gentle as a featherball with everyone he knew, raging and vicious at the sight or smell of strangers. How, sleuths wondered, had the murderer got past him?

Testing Jack, investigators sent a stranger to the front and rear doors of the house. Each time, Jack was furious at the very scent.

Therefore, police concluded, Jack either knew the murderer and hence didn't bother him, or else there was no murderer at all and Mrs. Haynes was indeed a suicide.

But the suicide theorists never explained the blinking lights, or Mrs. Haynes' two missing diamond rings.

Conversely, those whose opinions inclined to murder never managed to make an arrest.

SON INHERITED ESTATE

Much has changed in Knoxville since Mrs. Haynes' death. Her son, William P. Haynes, who inherited her entire estate, still lives here. But both the brooding Haynes home and the Haynes-Henson Shoe Co. are gone.

The son and daughter-in-law moved out of the house within a week of the murder and no one ever lived there again. The home was razed and the Northfield Apartments erected on the site in 1931. Even the street number left: 2310 Broadway is now five blocks nearer town and assigned to a doughnut shop.

The Haynes-Henson Shoe Co. went out of business during the Depression.

From the long perspective of 31 years, perhaps one of the shortest News-Sentinel editorials in history is as good an appraisal of the Haynes case as any. Said The News-Sentinel on May 6, 1929:

"The Haynes murder has all of the elements present in the great mystery stories of fiction.

"Except a good detective."

NEXT: Western Avenue Viaduct, death at each end for a cab driver.

April 26, 1959 issue of The Knoxville News-Sentinel detailing the Haynes "suicide or murder" story 30 years later.

dows of both rooms. Accompanied by his cousin, young Haynes climbed out his bedroom window and stepped quickly down the porch to the window of his mother's room. It was unlocked, and they went in.

"Mynatt turned on the lights," said William P. Haynes. "She was dead. There were two pools of blood and a stained knife beside her. A one ounce bottle of carbolic acid, two thirds empty, stood on the mantel. We called the police."

The police, Homicide Chief Harry Burke and Capt. John

11

Montgomery, arrived and started up the stairs with young Haynes and Mynatt. Mynatt had a shotgun. It went off accidentally and blew a hole in the floor. Burke and Montgomery, perhaps unnerved by the blast, made a quick inspection of the bedroom and the body.

They emerged and called the death a suicide.

Mrs. Renfro's comment on their work was pungent. "The most bungling piece of work," she said, "that I have ever seen."

Next day a coroner's jury agreed with Mrs. Renfro. Mrs. Haynes, said the jury, "came to her death by foul means at the hands of an unknown person."

Cook's Boyfriend Quizzed

Shifting their verdict nimbly from suicide to murder, the police went to work. They quizzed the cook.

She'd been out back in her own little house, said the cook, and noted nothing but the on-and-off twinkling of the lights.

They grilled Sloan McNabb, a friend of the cook, who said at first he'd dated the cook and then gone home. Finally he admitted spending the night with the cook. But he hadn't been in the house where Mrs. Haynes had locked herself in with the bulldog Jack.

They questioned Ed Fernand, a young civil engineer and a friend of William P. Haynes. Fernand owned a small car similar to one seen near the house by a passing streetcar rider.

But Fernand was clean.

Two weeks went by without a solid suspect. Investigative minds began to think again of suicide. In an effort to clear the air, William P. Haynes brought down a Philadelphia detective, Peter Sheller, to make a new investigation.

Sheller took a two-day look-see and pronounced Mrs. Haynes a suicide.

The sheriff agreed with him. The city safety director didn't. And who felt the full force of their quandary? The bulldog Jack.

Watchdog Passes Test

Jack, said all who knew him, was the model watchdog, gentle as a featherfall with everyone he knew, raging and vicious at the sight or smell of strangers. How, sleuths wondered, had the murderer got past him?

Testing Jack, investigators sent a stranger to the front and rear doors of the house. Each time, Jack was furious at the very scent.

Therefore, police concluded, Jack either knew the murderer and hence didn't bother him, or else there was no murderer at all and Mrs. Haynes was indeed a suicide.

But the suicide theorists never explained the blinking lights, or Mrs. Haynes' two missing diamond rings.

Conversely, those whose opinions inclined to murder never managed to make an arrest.

Son Inherited Estate

Much has changed in Knoxville since Mrs. Haynes' death. Her son, William P. Haynes, who inherited her entire estate, still lives here. But both the brooding Haynes home and the Haynes-Henson Shoe Co. are gone.

The son and daughter-in-law moved out of the house within a week of the murder and no one ever lived there again. The home was razed and the Northfield Apartments erected on the site in 1931. Even the street number left: 2310 Broadway is now five blocks nearer town and assigned to a doughnut shop.

The Haynes-Henson Shoe Co. went out of business during the Depression.

From the long perspective of 31 years, perhaps one of the shortest News-Sentinel editorials in history is as good an appraisal of the Haynes case as any. Said The News-Sentinel on May 6, 1928:

"The Haynes murder has all of the elements present in the great mystery stories of fiction.

"Except a good detective."

CHAPTER THREE

The Shadow People and a
Suspicious Death

*Unanswered questions still remain
in 88-year-old mystery*

Michael Williams
Haunted Knoxville Ghost Tours

In a Knoxville apartment complex more than one resident has reported encounters with a ghostly specter known as "The Shadow Person." The complex stands on the site that was the scene of a suspicious death that has left many unanswered questions nine decades later. In this story we will look back on the crime that rocked a city, the enduring mystery and the aftermath as well as the spectral appearances that suggests restless spirits calling out from the grave for justice.

Late in the evening of April 18, 1928, a crowd of onlookers gathered near a stately Haynes Estate located at 2310 Broadway in Knoxville, Tennessee, where police had arrived at a bloody death scene of Lillian Haynes.

Haynes was the matriarch of the Haynes family, one of Knoxville's most prominent. The suspicious nature of her death left many unanswered questions that continue to baffle arm chair detectives and historians 88 years after she was discovered by her son. Her death sent shockwaves through the community and cast a veil of suspicion on her son who labored intensively to prove his mother's death was in fact a suicide and not a murder as some had speculated. The circumstances and death scene led two law enforcement agencies to reach two polar opposite conclusions that were as different as night and day.

> The suspicious nature of her death left many unanswered questions that continue to baffle arm chair detectives and historians 88-years-after she was discovered by her son.

To modern historians the Haynes family emerges from the pages of local history as Knoxville's version of the Kennedy family. Like the Kennedy's, they were wealthy, well connected and had experienced their share of scandal and tragedy.

The Haynes family were heirs to a prosperous shoe company that was once located on Jackson Street where the JFG coffee house now stands.

Suspicious death of Lillian Haynes leaves unanswered questions

Lillian, affectionately known as Lillie, was married to William Paris Haynes Sr. The couple had two sons who had hoped to eventually inherit the family business. William Haynes Sr. had died several years prior at the age of 51 after suffering a long and lingering illness that left him crippled. The couple's younger

16

son, James, had a reputation around town for trouble with the law and racing automobiles down the streets of Knoxville. His flagrant disrespect for the law, heavy drinking, and his divorce brought scandal to the family in an era when divorce was relatively rare and frowned upon in the Bible Belt. Though he had remarried, his marital commitment had done nothing to rein in his wild life style. One afternoon in 1924, James was racing through town when he wrecked his car and suffered serious injuries. He never fully recovered from his injuries and died three years later in May of 1927, at the age of 28.

A year after James' death, tragedy struck the family again when long-time family friend and president of the Haynes Shoe Company, Oscar Tate, was found dead in the basement of the company.

With his death his brother, W.P. Jr. became the sole heir to the family fortune. Like his sibling, W.P. had his run-ins with the law and had been divorced. In 1928, one divorce in a family was scandalous, two in a family was a disgrace. Lillie Haynes was a highly respected member of the church and secretary treasurer of the Knox County Humane Society. Her sons' scandalous behavior was likely a source of embarrassment.

A year after James' death, tragedy struck the family again when long-time family friend and president of the Haynes Shoe Company, Oscar Tate, was found dead in the basement of the company. The death was a result of a self-inflicted gun-shot wound and ruled a suicide. His death struck many as odd as he had left no reason for ending his life.

A clan of scarred survivors lived in the estate. The grounds of the estate encompassed most of the city block. Inside the main house lived Lillian with her widowed daughter-in-law, her only surviving son and a bulldog named Jack. On the grounds of the home was a smaller house occupied by Mamie Siler, the family cook.

According to reports, on April 18, 1928, the last day of Lillian's life, she had spent the afternoon talking to her mother, Mrs. James Renfro, on the phone and looking through old family photos, sifting through memories. She seemed depressed as she spoke of her late husband and son.

At approximately 7 p.m. W.P. went out for the evening with his girlfriend to the Riviera Theater on Gay Street to see a minstrel show "The Blackville National Guards." Following the performance was a silent movie, a murder mystery entitled "A Night of Mystery."

He arrived home near midnight and went upstairs. He called out to his mother and there came no response. He attempted to enter her room but found her door locked and became alarmed. He called his cousin, E.F. Mynatt, who quickly arrived on the scene. The two stepped out onto the balcony and entered Lillian's bedroom from the balcony door. Mynatt turned on the lights and found Lillian lying on the floor dead.

Police were summoned and soon arrived on the scene which they found to be suspicious. Two detectives, Chief Harry Burke and Capt. John Montgomery were ascending the stairs with Mynatt who was carrying a shotgun. While ascending the stairs, the shotgun Mynatt was carrying went off, blasting a hole in the floor.

At the top of the stairs they inspected the death scene. There they found Lillian lying on the floor with her head near the hearth with her throat cut. A small stained dull paring knife lay nearby. Her necklace was broken and a small one ounce bottle of carbolic acid, two thirds empty, sat atop the mantle. Her face, mouth and eye had been splashed with acid. Her hair was neatly

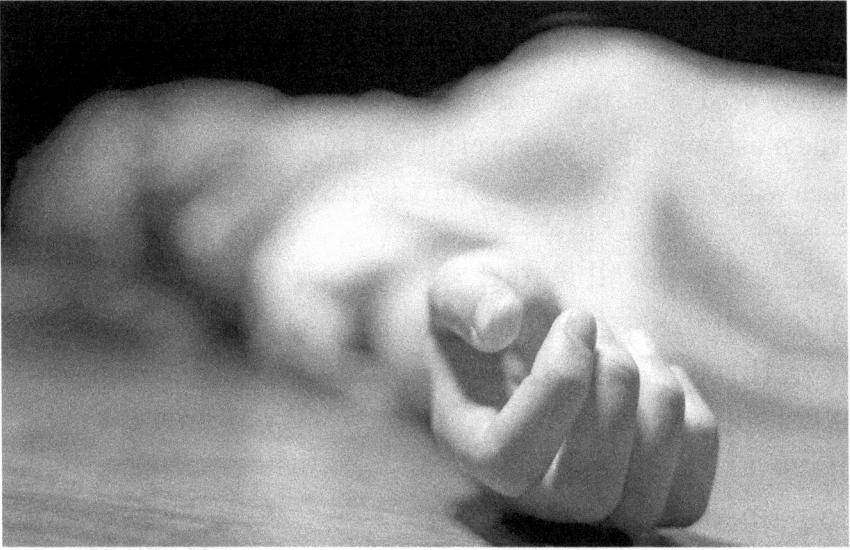

styled and two pools of blood pooled beside her. After a cursory examination of the crime scene the two detectives emerged and ruled the death a suicide reporting that Mrs. Haynes had cut her own throat.

The victim's mother, Mrs. Renfro, was astonished at the findings and quickly dismissed the investigation into her daughter's death as "The most bungling piece of work that I have ever seen." W.P. Haynes reportedly told Det. Burke that he believed robbers had entered his mother's home and slashed her throat while forcing acid into her mouth.

Disproving his theory was the fact that her room was left intact and no other valuables were taken.

The coroner John Scott ruled it the 12th suicide of the year. But then the dissenters joined ranks with Mrs. Renfro. Among them were detectives from the sheriff's department who considered the death a homicide. The following day, a coroner's jury agreed with Mrs. Renfro, calling Mrs. Haynes' demise "death by foul means at the hands of an unknown person."

At the behest of Mrs. Renfro and the coroner's jury the police began making a more thorough inquiry into Lillian's death. Many questions emerged. Why were two oil lamps, which were rarely used at the time, found burning outside her bedroom door? The most puzzling question of all was how could she burn her face with acid then slash her throat with a dull paring knife? While it is possible for a person to slash their own throat with a knife, a person would have to have a high threshold to pain and have a very sharp knife. Mrs. Haynes supposedly used a dull paring knife. Another question arose pertaining to her activities moments before her untimely death. Mrs. Haynes had completed a puzzle in the morning paper shortly before she died. If she were truly suicidal would she have taken the time to complete a puzzle?

> While it is possible for a person to slash their own throat with a knife, a person would have to have a high threshold to pain and have a very sharp knife.

Police interviewed Sloan McNabb, the boyfriend of the cook who was with her in her quarters the night of Mrs. Haynes death. Mamie told investigators she saw the lights come on in Mrs. Haynes' bedroom at approximately 8:40 and they went off again at 9 p.m. If Haynes had committed suicide how could she have turned off the lights?

A streetcar conductor that passed by the home on the night of the killing told police he had seen a car in front of the house parked awkwardly. The car turned out to belong to Ed Ferdnand, a civil engineer that had once worked for the family as a chauffeur. Ferdnand was questioned and never charged.

To quell any rumors, W.P. hired an outside detective from Philadelphia, Pennsylvania, named Peter Sheller to investigate. After two days he dismissed the death as a suicide.

Some suspected Mrs. Haynes was murdered by an insider.

Fueling this suspicion was the fact that she was found locked in her home alone with her dog, Jack who was gentle with his family but very aggressive and could be vicious with strangers. Jack would have likely attacked a stranger entering the home. This piece of information shifted the air of public suspicion on W.P. who was well known to the canine. As the sole heir to the fortune, W.P. had much to gain. The business and estate was worth $105,000. According to Save.org, $108,000 in 1928 dollars would be equivalent to $1,435,556.00 in 2016. Some suggested he had hired the detective and paid him off to rule the death a suicide after a sham investigation.

Life changed quickly for W.P. Within a week of his mother's death, he and his sister-in-law moved from the mansion and no one ever lived there again. For years locals whispered behind his back about his possible involvement in is mother's death. W.P. would not enjoy his prosperity for long. A year after he inherited the fortune the Great Depression derailed the American economy and the Haynes Shoe Company went bankrupt. The home was eventually razed and the land where it once stood became the site of a convalescent home and later an apartment complex.

W.P. Haynes never left town and died in Knoxville more than half a century later. But questions surrounding Mrs. Haynes death persist. As writer Lee Winfrey summed it up, "the Haynes murder has all the elements present in the great murder mystery stories of fiction except a good detective."

Beware the Shadow People: Restless Spirits on the site of the former Haynes Estate

In the 1930s through the 1950s, when the convalescent home operated on the site more deaths likely occurred among the sick and aging patients. This fact combined with the death of Mrs.

Haynes has spawned speculation that the site is now the permanent abode to many restless spirits. Among those is the ghost of Lillie Haynes reaching out from the grave seeking justice and vindication in her own demise.

The story of the mysterious death of Mrs. Haynes seems to be far from over. The apartment complex where her house once stood has been reported to have an ominous presence known as the Shadow person. The complex, which was named the Kentshires, has had numerous residents that have moved in and soon left the complex after experiencing what appears to be supernatural phenomenon.

Nationally renowned paranormal historian, J. Adam Smith, was familiar with the property and began gathering information about the site and investigated the haunted history. Smith, who has been deemed an expert in the field, owns and operates the Haunted Knoxville Ghost Tours. He has been featured on nationally televised shows such as "Paranormal Paparazzi" on the Travel Channel, hosted an Internet-based paranormal TV show and starred in a Telly Award winning paranormal documentary, "Historic Haunting: A Paranormal Study of Ramsey House." Smith connected the dots and discovered the tragic history of the complex. He interviewed residents, both past and present, and noted the events from the mysterious death of Mrs. Haynes and the succeeding years during which the property served as a convalescent home. Through diligent research Smith located a past resident who had several spine-chilling experiences that forced her to seek other living accommodations.

April W. moved into a small apartment at the Kentshires in 2012. In an October 2016 interview, she shared her experiences with those she refers to as "the Shadow People." She felt the rent was reasonable which would allow her to save some money. The complex was centrally located and in close proximity to her job at a nearby Mexican restaurant. Several of her co-workers lived there as well. Soon after moving in, April began hearing footsteps through her apartment.

She spoke to several co-workers that lived in the complex who each told her they heard footsteps in their apartments as well.

> One night, she began to fall asleep on her couch. Suddenly she was overcome by a feeling she was being watched.

Days later she heard what sounded like the front door opening followed by footsteps coming down the hallway to her bedroom.

One afternoon April watched her dog as he pursued an unseen presence. She observed the dog looking up as it followed an indiscernible manifestation. The dog finally came to the wall and reared upon on its hind legs reaching toward the ceiling with his fore paws. Smith was particularly intrigued by the pet's peculiar behavior.

"Animals are highly sensitive creatures," Smith said. "Throughout history they have had an awareness of seeing through the veil that separates the world of the living and the dead. I had a personal experience with a dog's behavior at a home I purchased in Florida that was uncharacteristic of the dog's typical behavior. He began growling in a protective nature at a wall. By recognizing the behavior as being protective, I decided to burn sage which calmed the animal down and improved the emotional energy within the home. Do not disregard your pet's behavior. It could be a sign of warning from them to you."

Soon afterwards April had an encounter with a spirit she refers to as "the Shadow Person." One night, she began to fall asleep on her couch. Suddenly she was overcome by a feeling she was being watched. She opened her eyes and in the corner of the room at the ceiling she saw what appeared to be a shadowy figure emerging from the ceiling. April described it as the figure of the upper torso of a person with its arms upraised coming toward her. April was frozen in fear and tried to scream but could barely utter a sound. Terrified she rolled off the couch and turned to look and the shadowy figure was gone but would be back.

"I became depressed," said April. "I didn't tell my friends about it because I didn't know if they would believe me. I wondered if I had dreamed the whole thing."

But April would soon discover she was not alone. Others would soon experience an otherworldly presence. April's parents came for a visit and spent the night with their daughter. The following morning April's mom had a disconcerting experience to relate.

"Mom told me she woke up with this eerie feeling that someone was watching her. She opened her eyes and saw a woman standing at the foot of her bed. She was wearing a white dress and she just stood there watching Mom," said April.

April's mother rolled over and buried her face in the pillow and tried to go back to sleep. But it proved to be a restless night. She reported hearing footsteps throughout the night and she and her husband left that day. She told April her apartment was "creepy" and suggested she find another place to live.

April was relieved to find that she wasn't the only one experiencing these ghostly visitations. But soon she had another visitation that prompted her to immediately make other living arrangements.

One afternoon she saw a man standing in her living room. He appeared to be an older man with a pale complexion and dark eyes. Without saying a word, the man turned and walked into the wall and vanished. After seeing the apparition vanish, April immediately left the apartment and began looking for another place to live.

"It was wise she moved out," said Smith. There are elements

of danger associated with living in a stigmatized property. I feel the most dangerous elements can be of emotional and psychological distress. On occasion, I have heard stories of people getting scratched during investigations, but I feel the most common effects in haunted locations are the emotions that are flying throughout the premises. April confided in me that after she moved out she experienced a change of night and day in her emotions."

Do the restless spirits of Lillian Haynes and her son still haunt the halls of the Kentshires? Is she attempting to reach out from the grave to tell the world the truth about her death? Who is the Shadow Person and who is the man April saw in her apartment? Does Oscar Tate's alleged suicide suggest any connection with the death of Mrs. Haynes?

"Who killed Mrs. Haynes is the million-dollar question," said Smith. "I find that the investigation has very shady elements. At the time that she died the law sometimes had a lack of accountability. There was a lot of money that was up for grabs. Especially seeing that Oscar Tate just happened to be found dead a little over a month before Lillian was found dead... With the advances in forensic science and new innovations in technology today, I would love for the police to reopen the case and use forensics and finger printing to find out what really happened that fateful night."

Knoxville Paranormal Historian Provides Valuable Insight Into *Ghostly Places in Tennessee*

By Kevin Slimp

Editor, Haunted Places in Tennessee

An afteroon spent with resident paranormal "guru" J. Adam Smith proved to be invaluable to completing *Ghostly Places in Tennessee.*

I spent the afternoon with J. Adam, listening as he shared stories of tours he has led and legends passed from generation to generation about possible hauntings in the Knoxville area.

J. Adam Smith
Haunted Knoxville Ghost Tours

J. Adam proved to be quite gracious, offering to help in any way he could. Many of the old stories from Knoxville newspapers were uncovered by J. and his team, making my job a lot easier.

When you're in the Knoxville area, be sure to check out hauntedknoxville.net for the schedule of upcoming ghost tours. If you're lucky, you might even find a tour guided by J. Adam himself.

CHAPTER FOUR

Knock, Knock
Nobody's There

The New Canton Knocking Spirit

By Joel Spears
The Rogersville Review

A drawing of the New Canton farmhouse where the knocking spirit was said to dwell. (File photo)

Icy, autumn winds nipped at Mamie Lou Bishop's home as she reminisced about a night long ago when an infamous knocking spirit many eastern Hawkins County residents can recall came tapping close to home.

Her story begins in the 1930s on a country road in the New Canton community. Curiosity had gotten the best of young Mamie Lou after hearing her sister Lide's tale of the mysterious poltergeist plaguing her uncle's house down the road.

"Me and Lide, that was my twin sister, went to hear the knocking spirit," Mamie began. "Lide had already been to hear it, so I said let's just go over and stay all night."

So, the two girls walked to the old farmhouse not far from Elm Springs Church, but Mamie got more than she expected once they were all tucked into their cousin's bed.

"I slept in the middle," she said with a chuckle. "I didn't want to sleep anywhere else because I already knew I'd came to hear this spirit."

Mamie's cousin knew what the girls came for too, but Mamie Lou still wasn't convinced the house was haunted, at least not at first.

"We were in my cousin's bed so I got her by the hands and held them, then seen that her feet didn't move. Then I was sure she wasn't making any racket," Mamie laughed.

It wasn't long though until the racket was obviously not in the bed, but outside the bedroom window.

"There was a corn crib up from the house and a little, old barn out from there where the family kept a mare named Old Nancy," Mamie recalled.

"When that spirit first come down it was like somebody took the back of an axe and hit a plank with it over and over. It just kept on and kept on."

Mamie's aunt was the first one to comment on the unusual

noise that had broken the dead silence in the room where the family's beds were.

"She said, 'I believe Old Nance is down out there in the barn'," Mamie remembered, but if it was the horse it kept clopping closer to the house with every beat.

Finally, it kept on without ceasing and entered the house through the wall, according to Mamie Lou.

"My uncle said, 'That thing's come back again tonight and we won't sleep none.'"

When the specter entered into the room, Mamie and the rest of the family were wide awake and the girls were curious to ask the spirit a few questions.

"We went to asking it things, 'yes' and 'no' questions, and it would peck them off," Mamie said pecking at the end table beside her chair. "I'm not lying about that either.

"Finally, the thing went across the room. It sounded like something running down a big rope or a big, stout wire from the corner of the room, then come slanting down to the middle of the room," she said.

Another bed sat across the room from the girls, near the fireplace where the spirit landed.

"When that thing come sliding down you could hear it hit the bed like it was beating it with an axe. It didn't do anything to the bed though," she said with a look of seriousness in her eyes.

As Mamie continued her tale, the look of genuine faith in having heard the unexplainable became more evident on her face. She knows what she heard that night.

"You could tell it was in there," she said. "After it hit the bed you could hear it walking, just like a little old woman or man under our bed. It walked around until finally it got under our pillow and you could feel the sound tapping under our heads." But the girls didn't mind.

29

"We kept on laughing and aggravating the thing with questions and it would peck off answers every time," she said.

Mamie never mentioned whether or not she ever stayed all night in her uncle's house again, but the knocking spirit made itself at home.

"My uncle said he got up many a morning to build a fire and the spirit made sounds like little women with high heel shoes who would give the door a big knock," she said. "It would open and close, but nobody would see a thing. Then the safe where they kept the dishes in would make a sound like everything in it broke too, but nothing was ever out of place.

"They never did know what it was," Mamie said reflectively. "This is all the plain truth. People from all around went there to hear that thing knock. Papa didn't believe it, then went there and was afraid of it.

"I didn't believe it, until I'd heard it for myself," she said sternly. "It was like the devil. There was nothing they could do to even move away from it. It had to be the devil's work because I don't think the Lord would have played no trick like that. For all I know the thing may still be over in there now.

This story originally appeared in the October 29/30, 2005 edition of the The Rogersville Review. Its storyteller, Mamie Lou Bishop (pictured), passed away on May 11, 2010. This story is dedicated to her memory. (Photo by Joel Spears)

CHAPTER FIVE

Most Haunted Places
in McNairy County

With Ghost Hunter, Roger Hill

By Christen Coulon
Independent Appeal (Selmer)
October 15, 2014

Local Ghost Hunter Roger Hill sat down with the Independent Appeal last week to discuss the field of ghost hunting and share some of his experiences at the most haunted locations within McNairy County.

Hill said that he has been fascinated with ghosts since he was a child growing up in a haunted house in Bethel Springs.

"Of course, we didn't know it was haunted until I was 11 or 12 years old," Hill said. "We shot at people, or at least, we thought it was people. It was an old house and it was probably about 100 years old then in the 1950s."

Hill said that they thought people were trying to get into their home because they could see someone (or something) twisting the door knob from the opposite side of the door on many occa-

Roger Hill

G.H.O.S.T. Hunters of Southern Tennessee

sions. But when they would investigate, no one was ever there.

Later, as Hill grew into a teen, he said that he began to see ghostly apparitions and he described an unusual room in the home which was always cold.

It was these experiences as a child which drove Hill to continue searching for answers as an adult. As he researched the field, he began picking up ghost hunting equipment, and eventually went on to form G.H.O.S.T. (Ghost Hunters of Southern Tennessee).

Hill said that in the 1950s and 1960s researchers began using equipment to capture EVP (electronic voice phenomena) recordings. Hill said that the field has changed a lot in the past few decades as ghost hunters have begun to use sensitive scientific equipment to aid them in their search for the unexplained.

Today, Hill said that ghost hunters have trunks of equipment and use devices such as digital audio and video recorders, EMF (electromagnetic field) meters, laser grid projectors, infrared cameras and thermometers, and a device known as a spirit box. A spirit box is simply a radio rigged to cycle through frequencies at a rate of about four per second.

And while ghost hunters of the past relied mostly on personal observations, ending their hunts when they left the location they were researching, much has changed. Hill said that today, hunters will sift through the recordings and measurements after a hunt to see if they were able to capture anything that escaped the ability of their senses to detect during the hunt itself. In addition, most hunters will also come equipped with an array of personal communication devices, flashlights, first aid kits, and even computers while in the field. Hill's group, G.H.O.S.T. is comprised of about 12-15 members, many of whom have been conducting hunts around this region for years.

Hill said on average, a hunt will consist of about 8-10 people. The group has been on an extended break this year, but Hill said that following Halloween they plan to go on some additional hunts in the area.

Hill said that the first hunt will likely be a return to the Hurst Mansion in Purdy, the location which Hill says is the most haunted place he has witnessed in the county. The Hurst Mansion is not the only haunted location in the county, Hill said. One of the most haunted locations outside the mansion, however, ironically is also related to the Hurst legend.

Hill discussed a site in the northern end of the county which formerly lay on a road from Purdy to Jackson, Tenn. Hill said that the site's former owners who lived there during the Civil

War killed their slaves in a fire in an attempt to avoid being captured by Union troops.

"When you get close to this place you can feel it," Hill said. "They knew that (Hurst) was probably going to come through and burn their places and free the slaves." Hill said that his group did not capture any

EVPs, but said that it was something you can feel when you get near the property.

"There is no question that it is haunted," Hill said.

Hill said that G.H.O.S.T. is looking at other investigations around the county including a small property on the western end of the county which the owner has said is haunted.

G.H.O.S.T
Ghost Hunters
of
Southern
Tennessee

CHAPTER SIX

The
Thomas House

Historical Macon County Landmark
Draws Paranormal Interest

By: Jessie Ellefson
Macon County Chronicle
September 25, 2012

The historic Thomas House Hotel, located in Red Boiling Springs, offers more to guests than your average, run-of-the-mill overnight stay.

Drawing guests interested in a history lesson and the opportunity to step back in time, the 122-year-old hotel has also become known for the paranormal activities experienced by many of those who have spent the night in one of the hotel's 14 rooms.

Featured on the A&E Network's nationally broadcast television show *Paranormal State* in their third season's line-up, the Thomas House was investigated by The Paranormal Research Society (PRS), founded by Penn State student Ryan Buell in 2001.

The episode, entitled "Room 37," premiered on April 13, 2009, and since its airing has become a retreat for those intrigued by the unknowns of the paranormal world.

Earlier this year, the hotel was featured on the Syfy Channel's wildly popular *Ghost Hunters* television series. The show features Jason Hawes and Grant Wilson - plumbers by day and ghost hunters by night – who, along with their team, work to track down the presence of paranormals across the country and either embrace or 'de-bunk' their existence.

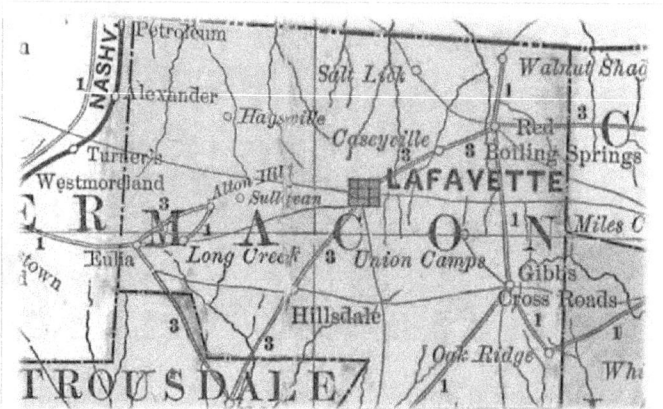

Some of the most talked about supernatural stories that have emerged from the hotel over the years include tales about a former cook who still remains in the room he once lived in, a whistling man who walks the halls during the day, a gentleman who haunts the front desk where guests check in and a little girl believed to be named Sara, who died at the hotel when she was brought to the town for the healing waters.

The hotel itself, has endured its share of tragedy, including two fires. Historically, it became a popular summer destination after word spread across the country that the small town of Red Boiling Springs had mineral waters that contained medicinal qualities and it was perhaps best known for its luxurious hotels and bathhouses, which among the notables of famous people included President Woodrow Wilson, who spent his summers there.

Formerly the Cloyd Hotel, the Cole Family (Cherry, Darrell, Evelyn & David) purchased the Thomas House Hotel in 1993, keeping the classic, inviting style of the hotel intact and adding their own special touches to the experiences available to guests.

Offering a dinner theatre production two weekends in every month, a Sunday dinner buffet, an antique shop, museum room memorabilia displays, and family style lunch and dinners Monday through Saturday (by reservation), guests not only come for the inviting atmosphere but also for the entertainment and one-of-a-kind dining experience.

For more information contact the Thomas House Hotel at 699-300-6520 or stop by 520 Main St. in Red Boiling Springs and see this Macon County landmark for yourself!

This is Historic Westwood House in Knoxville. See
the photo of the mysterious figure taken in this house
by Knoxville author Janena White on page 104.

CHAPTER SEVEN

The
Bell Witch

*Historical Macon County Landmark
Draws Paranormal Interest*

By Kevin Slimp
The Newspaper Institute

John and Lucy Bell, along with their nine children, moved their belongings, including a number of slaves, from North Carolina to Tennessee around 1804. Eventually, the Bell farm grew to more than 300 acres.

Before 1820, the Bells began to experience unexplained ghostly activieis centered around their daughter Betsy. These included a faint singing voice of an old woman, along with faint tappings. The Bell children were often awakened at night by something pulling at their bedcovers. They also reported hearing the sound of something chewing on the bedposts.

John Bell often described his encounters with a strange animal on this farm. He described the animal as having the head of a rabbit and the body of a dog. Though several hunting expeditions were held, the animal was never caught.

In addition, pounding noises were heard outside the house at night and Betsy was attacked in her sleep. She had the scars on her face to prove the beatings.

> In addition, pounding noises were heard outside the house at night and Betsy was attacked in her sleep. She had the scars on her face to prove the beatings.

Visitors to the home reported noises and moving objects. Eventually, the family recognized the words of the voice as someone reading scripture.

Eventually the voice began addressing family members by name. The voice hated John and warned his wife against marrying her lover.

John Bell was excommunicated from his church in 1818 as the story traveled throughout the community. Officially, the charge was usury over a slave sale, but it has long been believed by many that the supernatural events were the actual reason for his excommunication.

In one famous story, General Andrew Jackson visited the homestead in 1819, to visit the Bell sons who served under him during the Battle of New Orleans. He had heard the tales of the

The family of John Bell lived on a farm near Adams, Tennessee, in the early 1800s. In the centuries since, the legend of the Bell Witch has been passed from generation to generation. How could such paranormal activity exist around the lives of such a "normal" family?

"Bell Witch," and wanted to investigate the stories for himself.

It was reported that Jackson had a horse-drawn wagon and several soldiers accompanying him. While approaching the farm, the wagon stopped and the horses were unable to move.

After unsuccessfully getting the wagon to move, Jackson shouted, "By the eternal, boys, it is the witch."

It was then, according to accounts at the time, a female voice was heard, saying "All right General. Let the wagon move on. I will see you again tonight."

According to the legend, the horses were immediately able to make their way. Jackson had planned to stay several nights, as the story goes, but changed his mind after several encounters with the witch on his initial evening.

Written accounts exist of Jackson's visit, but the story does not appear in any of Jackson's personal essays.

Over time, John Bell began referring to the witch as "Kate." Throughout his life, the sounds and visits continued. John Bell died in 1820 at the age of 70, and it is told that the family found a mysterious vial in the room where Bell's body rested.

To test the contents, they allowed the family cat to drink the contents of the vial, and it immediately died. Then, according to the legend, the witch spoke and took credit for Bell's death..

It's even told the witch sang and laughed during the burial of Bell. In 1828, "Kate" made her final appearance, in a conversation with John Bell, Jr. Accounts of the discussion describe an upcoming "Civil War" in the United States.

Details of the Bell Witch vary, as the account wasn't written until the story appeared in a book in 1894.

It is often speculated that the manifestations may have been a ruse to convince Betsy Bell to break off the impending marriage to her fiancé Joshua Gardner. Betsy eventually ended the relationship, which was opposed by the witch, in 1821.

In 1824, she married Richard Powell, her teacher. Some Believe Powell may have caused the initial manifestations. Powell was a frequent visitor to the Bell home and took a quick liking to Betsy. It wasn't long after that the mysterious noises began.

The Bell Witch still brings chills to the spines of many who visit the area where the haunting is said to have taken place.

CHAPTER EIGHT

The Haunting of Sensabaugh Tunnel

Some say the tunnel is still haunted

By Jessica Kelly
Hawkins Today Reporter

KINGSPORT – The Sensabaugh Tunnel, built around 1909 in the Kingsport area of Hawkins County to accommodate the railroad passing through the valley, has an eerie past, according to urban legend. At least two urban legends regarding the tunnel have developed throughout the years.

Sensabaugh Tunnel

According to the first legend, a hobo had wandered to the home of the Sensabaugh family and was welcomed into the home. At some point the hobo reportedly attempted to steal jewelry from the family. When Mr. Sensabaugh saw what the hobo was trying to do, he grabbed his pistol and pointed it at the hobo.

The hobo allegedly grabbed the couple's baby and used it to shield himself from the pistol as he fled out the door. According to the legend the hobo was able to outrun Mr. Sensabaugh and fled into the tunnel. Not knowing what to do with the baby, he allegedly drowned it in the creek which flows through the tunnel. As with many urban legends, there is more than one version of the story.

According to another legend, Sensabaugh lived with his family near the entrance of the tunnel in a white house. One day Sensabaugh reportedly went crazy and murdered his family, including the youngest child, who was a baby. Sensabaugh then reportedly threw their bodies into the creek that runs through the tunnel. While very different stories, both have one common factor, the death of a baby.

John, Dora and Roger Sensabaugh, taken in 1955.

Some say the tunnel is still haunted by the eerie cries of the infant and today people still drive to the tunnel in hopes of hearing those cries for themselves. They often drive into the tunnel, turn off the headlights, silence the sound of their engine and wait. Some claim to have heard the baby's cries. Others claim to have heard or seen much more.

In some accounts people claimed their car would not start again. In others they heard Mr. Sensabaugh's footsteps echoing in the tunnel or saw him appear in the rearview mirror of the car. There have also been claims of a handprint of a baby being left on the windshield of a car. Still others say they didn't hear or see anything while in the tunnel. There also seems to be some confusion as to which of two tunnels the legends belong to.

There are two tunnels and water flows through both. One can be driven through, while the other only has a foot path which runs along the left side of the tunnel. People have claimed to have had experiences in both. The drive-through tunnel is closest to the Sensabaugh's homeplace.

The tunnel was built in 1909, which begs the question, was the legend referring to John Sensabaugh (father) or Edward Sensabaugh (son)?

John built the house that is mentioned in the legend somewhere between 1889 and 1898, according to Roger Sensabaugh, his grandson. John and his wife Dora had

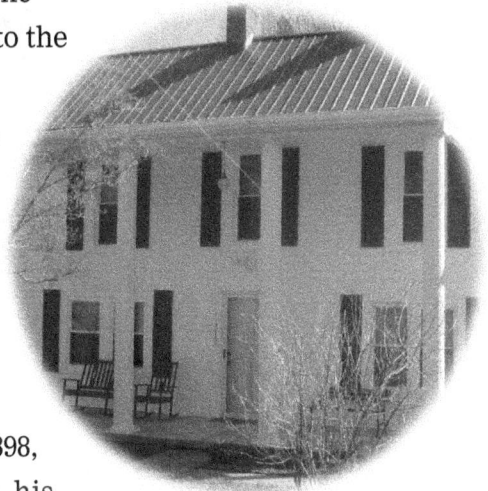

The Sensabaugh home.

four children and Edward was the youngest of the four, which would have made him the baby the legend spoke of. While no one really knows how these legends began, Roger said he believes the legend was referring to his dad, Edward, because he doesn't recall hearing any of these stories until around the age of 20. If the legend was referring to Edward, then the baby in question would be Roger.

"I don't know how it all started, but it's not true, or I wouldn't be here because I am his only child," said Roger.

He said if he had to guess how the legends started then he believes it would have been during the time when people started

45

parking inside and hanging around the tunnel. He said he remembers once when some people were parked inside the tunnel and his father decided to have some fun with them. He said his dad crept up to the tunnel, sat along the side of it, and began making the sounds of a baby crying.

"Dad was real good at making those noises," said Roger. "I know he is in the hereafter still having a laugh about it."

CHAPTER NINE

Captain Clay's
Black Horse

Fortune-teller of death?

A black riderless horse is said to have appeared the evening before Captain Henry Clay died.

By Mike Williams

The Rogersville Review

Does the loyal steed of a Civil War officer foretell the death of his descendants?

The Clay-Kenner mansion is one of the most historic buildings in Rogersville. The nearly 170-year-old ante-bellum home has also been the subject of numerous ghostly speculations over the years. There were reports of mysterious lights seen in the mansion in the 1960s and 1970s, a time when it stood empty and dilapidated. It has been suggested the lights were little more than flashlight beams belonging to vandals and trespassers.

Others have claimed the stairs are blood-stained. An examination with the naked eye proves otherwise. Wispy, mysterious figures have been sighted wandering the grounds between the trees. But is there anything to any of these suggestions of specters?

The most famous of the ghostly tales associated with the Clay-Kenner home, and perhaps most believable, focuses on a riderless black horse.

During the Civil War the mansion was home to Nancy Bynum, a young widow and loyal Confederate. She and her family had a secret room constructed in the cellar for the purpose of hiding valuables in the war years. It turned out the secret chamber saved a life.

Confederate General John Hunt Morgan and his men, among them Captain Henry Boyle Clay, visited Rogersville around this time. Clay and Bynum fancied one another and began courting.

In September of 1864 General Morgan was caught and executed by Union soldiers, his body dragged through the streets of Greeneville. Clay, with many of the general's men, was also ambushed. Clay narrowly escaped and made his way to

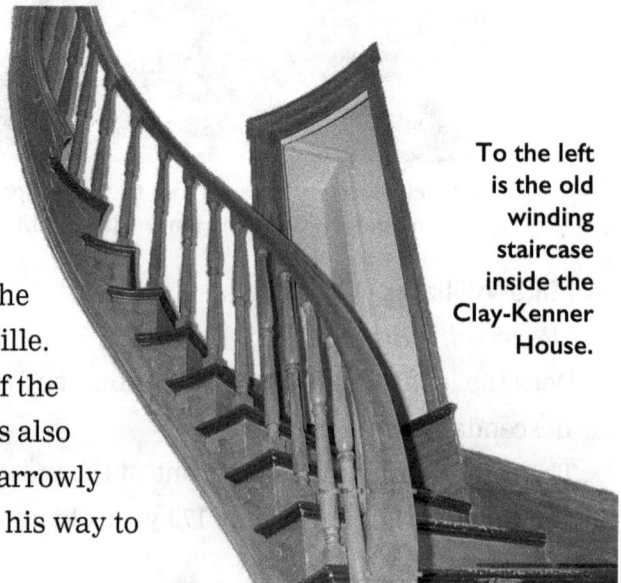

To the left is the old winding staircase inside the Clay-Kenner House.

Rogersville with his black horse.

In the attack Clay had been wounded. He was too weak to travel to his home in Kentucky and instead fled to be with the woman he loved.

Ceiling damage at the Clay-Kenner House, which has through the years fallen into disrepair.

Nancy Bynum hid her beloved captain in the secret chamber in the cellar as he convalesced. He slept on a bed of straw and had nothing but a small candle for light. A servant hid Clay's midnight-black horse in a back cellar until the captain was well enough to travel.

Legend says Clay escaped Union soldiers by using a secret network of passages under the mansion. Supposedly, the tunnels were constructed to allow escape from possible Indian attack years earlier. After the war Clay and Bynum married, raised a family and made their home in Rogersville.

Captain Clay died in 1919. The night before the captain's death, however, several folks said they witnessed a riderless black horse, scratching at the earth and neighing. Come morning the captain was dead and the black horse was gone.

A riderless black horse became an omen to the Clay family, appearing before the deaths of family members. Many folks have claimed to have spied the shadowy black beauty over the years. The last sighting was reported in 1957 prior to the death of Mary Clay Kenner.

Years later people claimed the network of tunnels under the Clay-Kenner home was actually part of the Underground Railroad and that nearly 50 slaves had been able to escape by hiding there. This is unlikely, considering the Bynum and Clay families' devotion to the Confederacy.

In the 1950s the tunnels were sealed off when they began caving in. The secret chamber in which Clay was hidden was discovered in the late 1970s when the home was under-going renovations. It was little more than a yawning cavity, and showed signs of collapse.

Today, the Clay-Kenner House stands empty, pending resto-

The Clay-Kenner mansion is one of the most historic buildings in Rogersville. The 170-plus-year-old antebellum home has also been the subject of numerous ghostly speculations over the years.

ration, but its attachment to its past and the supernatural are forever present. The house is currently the starting point of a commercial ghost walk through Historic Rogersville.

CHAPTER TEN

A Soldier's Experience
in the Tennessee Mountains

*Original story told in 1888
by Lt. A.L. Soule*

By Ken Coffey
Grainger Today

In late October I thought it would be interesting to share a story that was given to me from Blaine resident Heidi Steeves. This story appeared in the National Tribune in Washington, D.C., February 3, 1888, and was written by Lt. A.L. Soule.

— Ken Coffey

It was often remarked during the war that the soldiers of the rebellion, unlike others, were remarkably free of superstition. The time of which I write was in June, 1864, which was during the darkest days of the rebellion. I was then a Lieutenant, in command of Co. G 10th Mich. Cav. I had marched across the mountains from Camp Nelson, Kentucky, to Knoxville, Tennessee. The city and the country for miles was utterly devastated. Both armies had been compelled to subsist principally off the poor, mountain environed country, which, at best, could barely sustain its inhabitants. My regiment was stationed at Strawberry Plains, 16 miles west of Knoxville, where the East Tennessee and Virginia Railroad crosses the Holston River. The railroad bridge was an important outpost in the defense of Knoxville. Marauding bands of guerrillas protected by the mountain fastnesses were constantly making incursions into the settlements, plundering and murdering the guise of any role that best suited the circumstances.

North and east of Strawberry Plains, and about 10 miles distant, was a spot called Blaine's Crossroads. I call it a spot, be-

> The doors and windows were gone, the floors and parts of the casings were torn loose and scattered about, the plaster hung in shreds from the shattered walls, and in what I judge to have been the sitting room was a dried carcass of a dead horse.

December, 1863. Bridge at Strawberry Plains, 20 miles northeast of Knoxville.

cause there was nothing there but an old war-wrecked house, and instead of the roads crossing, they simply forked, one leading up the valley towards Rogersville and the other angling to the left in the direction of Cumberland Gap.

For some reason, which I could not question, our Colonel had conceived the idea that this crossroad was the key to his position on the north side of the Holston, and on the morning of June 15 I was ordered, with my company, with instructions to picket the roads, patrol the country, keep my company well in hand.

In my own mind I was satisfied that I understood the military situation in Tennessee, as well as the Colonel. Arriving at the crossroads, I found, as I have stated, the old house and the forks in the road. The house standing in the forks was a large two-story frame building and showed that at some time it had been quite an imposing structure. About it were the charred remains

53

of outbuildings. The doors and windows were gone, the floors and parts of the casings were torn loose and scattered about, the plaster hung in shreds from the shattered walls, and in what I judge to have been the sitting room was a dried carcass of a dead horse. Around what seemed to have been the yards and pleasure grounds was grown up with weeds and briars. There was no fence left standing, shade and fruit trees had fallen by the same hands that made Blaine's Crossroads. I thought if ghost and hob-goblin ever held high revel on earth, I had found the place.

About 10 o'clock I became nervous and walked out to the road, the occasional chirp of a cricket or call of a katydid startled me strangely.

I sent out patrols on the two roads with orders to proceed eight to 10 miles, get what information they could and return by nightfall. I have mentioned a dense growth of scrub oak that extended for a long distance north and south on either side of the road, the road ran nearly straight for about half a mile. I saw at a glance that the place for my picket was a short distance west of an elevation, as an object approaching from the front on reaching the crest would be clearly outlined against the sky. The patrols returned and reported nothing alarming.

The guard was in the charge of a trusty Sergeant and every-thing promised a quiet night. On the east side of the house was a wing or "L" containing one large room, which had probably been the kitchen, and in that the men gathered, with their horses picketed outside. A small fire, for light only, flickered from the ground in the center of the room, casting weird and ghostly shad-ows through the many cracks and crannies of the building.

Outside, the night was dark, but not so dark that an object could not be plainly seen against the sky. There was not the

Blaine Cafe near the spot at Blaine's Crossroads. Mr. Corum is depicted speaking to a gentleman in front of Rube Morgans's cafe.

slightest breath of air moving. About 10 o'clock I became nervous and walked out to the road, the occasional chirp of a cricket or call of a katydid startled me strangely. I returned to the house and seated myself in the circle. I cast my eyes around the circle of armed men and saw no inclination among them to sleep, when with a crash that seemed to fairly raise the roof from the old house and brought every man to his feet like an electric shock came the report of a gun from the direction of the picket on the valley road. Before the echoes had died away among the surrounding hills, the Sergeant, with his detail, was on his way to the relief of the post.

There was no repetition of the shot, and soon the Sergeant returned and reported that Williams, the picket, claimed to have seen a horseman approach from the front, and when he had reached the summit of the elevation, so as to be clearly seen against the sky, he had challenged him, and as he continued to advance, had fired. When the smoke cleared nothing could be seen of the horseman, nor had he heard the slightest sound of a footfall either before or after the shot. I remarked that Williams had probably drowsed and his imagination had gotten the better of him. It had probably been 20 minutes since the first alarms when again, with the same stunning report, and with like results, came another alarm from the same post. This time on his return the Sergeant brought in Williams, having placed in his stead a man named Thompson.

"I had just passed the little hill a few rods this side of the Blaine House, where lying in the road, with his faithful horse standing a silent watch, I found the dead body of the young Union soldier from Rogersville, shot through the heart."

Thompson was a burly, daredevil fellow, who was known by every man in the regiment to be absolutely devoid of fear. The Sergeant remarked, "If the devil rode that horse he would find his match now."

I questioned Williams closely, he told me the horseman twice had appeared between him and the sky, and twice disappeared without a sound when he had fired. He said nothing on earth would induce him to go back. Quiet had again settled down in our little camp. Thompson had been out not longer than 20 minutes when, to the utter consternation of every man, the third alarm boomed out, this time I ran with the Sergeant to the post.

Thompson told the same story. I told the Sergeant to return to camp and I would remain with Thompson. We took our position side by side in the middle of the road, facing east. The sky could be plainly seen above the low trees. Thompson in a hoarse whisper almost gasped, "There it comes, Lieutenant," and before I could collect my senses he had cried, "Halt," and instantly raised his gun and fired. I must have been deathly pale, for my knees smote together. I had no desire to investigate the matter further. I placed a Sergeant and 10 men at the post and the remainder of the night was passed without incident.

When I refreshed myself with a cup of coffee it occurred to me that the Sergeant in charge of the valley road had mentioned a family named Shields, living at the foot of the slope near the creek. I was determined to ride over to the house and learn, if possible, something of the area where we camp. I found Mr. Shields a man of more than ordinary intelligence. His age and infirmities had exempted him from the sweeping conscription of the confederacy and allowed him to remain at home, which I considered rather remarkable from the fact of his being with his mouth, a man of decided Union proclivities. I made no mention of what had transpired the night before and he told me, "About eight years before the war Henry Blaine had come from North Carolina and bought a large tract of land. The only family he brought was his daughter. She had matured into a beautiful woman when the war came. The son of a judge from Rogersville, received her brightest smiles. Mr. Blaine was a southern gentleman and when the young man accepted a captaincy in a Union Tennessee regiment, she was told not to see him again.

"One summer morning he rode through Blaine's Crossroads and planned a visit with his old sweetheart. The next day I had a note fall due against a man living about 20 miles over in Powell Valley and as times were getting so unsettled I thought I would go collect. Before the day had fairly dawned I mounted my horse and was on the road. My route was by the way of the crossroads and the Cumberland Gap Fork. I had just passed the little hill a few rods this side of the Blaine House, where lying in the road, with his faithful horse standing a silent watch, I found the dead body of the young Union soldier from Rogersville, shot through the heart."

I asked Mr. Shields if he knew the date this happened. "Yes," he replied, "I still have the note, due June 16, 1861."

"Miss Blaine only survived the tragic death of her boyfriend a few months. Mr. Blaine soon afterward went to the war and was killed at the battle of Chickamauga," he said.

CHAPTER ELEVEN

Finding Spirits in Greeneville

Ghost hunter claims he found evidence of spirits at D-W Mansion

By Tom Yancey
The Greeneville Sun
April 1, 2006

Stacey Allen McGee, a self-described "certified ghost hunter" who operates a company he calls Appalachian Ghostwalks, visited the Dickson-Williams Mansion Thursday night.

By the time he gathered his gear and left several hours later, McGee claimed to have found considerable evidence that the almost-190-year-old mansion is . . . haunted.

For two years now, McGee has conducted what he calls "hauntingly historic" guided, lantern-lit walking tours, or "ghost walks," that now include historic Jonesborough and Erwin, Buffalo Mountain and the campus of East Tennessee State University in Johnson City, and Abingdon, Va.

He is in the process of developing a similar walk in Greeneville, and hopes to start June 1, he said.

That "ghost walk," he says, will be called "Haunted Historic Greeneville." The cost of a walking tour will be $7 per person in groups of five or more.

> "In this context, he maintained, a vortex indicates where 'people from other times' may be able to enter the present.

Appalachian Ghostwalks, based in the small community of Unicoi, a few miles from Erwin, is a member of the Unicoi County Chamber of Commerce and the Northeast Tennessee Tourism Association (NETTA).

The business has a great deal of information, much of it historical in nature, on its Internet site, www.appalachianGhostWalks.com.

Limestone Native

McGee, a Limestone native who has spent most of his adult life in the hospitality industry, said in an interview that he believes "ghost walks" can be an important tourism

draw for the entire East Tennessee region, based on responses to the tours his group has conducted so far.

Sarah Webster, chairman of the Dickson-Williams Historical Association, said that when McGee approached that organization about conducting "scientific sweeps" of the historic house museum, the association was willing to cooperate.

Webster, along with Nancy McNeese, director of Main Street:

Greeneville, and McNeese's daughter-in-law, Anna Jeffers, who has experience with walking tours in historic Charleston, S.C., helped McGee conduct five "sweeps" of the building Thursday evening.

As a gesture of good faith, McGee presented the mansion association with an electronic page-scanned copy of Tennessee: A History, written by Dr. Philip Hamer, former chairman of the University of Tennessee's department of history.

Webster said the copy would be placed in the T. Elmer Cox Historical and Genealogical Library, where the public can have access to it.

In exchange, McGee was loaned a copy of Greeneville: 100 Year Portrait, 1775-1875, by the late local historian Richard H. Doughty, the driving force in the restoration of the 1820s-era brick mansion at the corner of N. Irish and W. Church streets.

The structure was the showplace residence of Dr. and Mrs. Alexander Williams from the early 1820s until after the Civil War. Famed Confederate Gen. John Hunt Morgan spent the last night of his life as a guest in the house in September 1864.

Later used as an inn, and even a factory, it was converted to use as the major part of the former Greeneville Hospital during most of the last century.

McGee said historical information from Doughty's book will be invaluable in preparing the "script" for the "ghost walk" tour.

Sun Photo by Phil Gentry
The Dickson-Williams Mansion is located on North Irish Street in downtown Greeneville.

Webster said people visit historic sites like the Dickson-Williams mansion for a variety of reasons, some of them very speculative, such as stories about unsolved mysteries.

She said the association is hopeful that people who learn about the house-museum from taking a "ghost walk" will be intrigued enough to want to take a separate tour of the mansion itself, and perhaps visit other historic sites in and around Greeneville as well.

Methods Explained

McGee explained the methods he uses to a Greeneville Sun reporter early Thursday evening, but he was unwilling to have the reporter present while the sweeps through the mansion were made.

The sweeps, he said, "are difficult to do when you also have to think about your public image."

The first sweep, he said, involved taking numerous digital photographs, using four different cameras.

The second sweep, he said, involved taking infrared photos. Infrared photos are expensive, he said, and thus are used sparingly.

For the third sweep he used a hand-held meter that indicates the presence of high electro-magnetic interference, which he said "we find typically in haunted locations."

Hall, Greeneville Sanatorium and Hospital, Greeneville, Tenn.

Electromagnetic interference usually does not mean very much when it's in a wall, McGee said, but when it's in the middle of a room, and is stationary, "We call it, for lack of a bet-

Stacey Allen McGee (left), of Appalachian GhostWalks, demonstrates the use of dowling rods he uses as one technique he said is successful in determining the presence of ghosts. Looking on are Sarah Webster (center), president of the Dickson-Williams Historical Association, and Anna Jeffers, who has experience with historical walking tours in Charleston, S.C. McGee said his investigation of the mansion Thursday evening showed that 27 ghosts or spirits are present there on a regular basis.

ter word, a vortex."

In this context, he maintained, a vortex indicates where "people from other times" may be able to enter the present.

27 Ghosts Or Spirits

McGee carefully avoids using words such as "dead" or "dead people."

But he was willing to state after visiting the mansion that his "sweeps" found evidence of "27 different ghosts or spirits

63

that haunt there on a regular basis."

McGee said he intentionally did not investigate the history of the mansion in depth before Thursday evening's "sweeps," in order

to be able to approach the site with an open mind.

He said a scan by him of the house museum's exterior during a preliminary tour of historic structures in Greeneville showed considerable supernatural activity at the Dickson-Williams mansion.

He emphasized that he did not trespass to make the initial observation, but also said that he is willing to perform the same type of "sweeps" at no charge in any historic home or structure in Greeneville or nearby.

McNeese said McGee was not surprised when told that the mansion was for many years part of a hospital. He told her that hospitals are often haunted.

The same is true of some college campuses, he added.

Peculiar Happenings?

The fourth sweep he conducted was an audio recording, which will later be subjected to acoustic analysis, McGee said.

During this sweep, McNeese and Webster said everyone present heard what sounded like footsteps on an upper floor, although no one was present there.

At another point, after McGee invited ghosts to "make themselves known," McNeese said window blinds on an upper floor began to rattle as if the window were open, though an investigation showed it was not, and no wind could be felt.

The fifth sweep, and the one that McGee said he believes is the most indicative of the presence of ghosts, is "dowsing," a very old method typically used to find underground water, but also used to find any number of other buried objects.

About Dowsing

Dowsing has both its advocates and its skeptics, as a quick Internet search will reveal.

Dowsing is a method, at least several thousand years old, in which a dowsing rod, dowsing stick or even a forked tree limb is used by the "dowser" holding it to try to locate an object.

McGee uses two narrow, metal, L-shaped rods to ask a series of yes-or-no questions, mostly about ghosts.

"Dowsing is not necessarily scientific," McGee acknowledged. But he also stated that between 85 and 90 percent of the ghost presences he says he has been able to identify in the region using that method have been verified from what history also says about structures where the method has been used.

> "Dowsing is not necessarily scientific," McGee acknowledged. But he also stated that between 85 and 90 percent of the ghost presences he says he has been able to identify in the region using that method."

McGee also said the University of Tennessee forensic medicine unit "employs dowsing to locate lost gravesites," with similar success.

McNeese said that, although the sweeps took several hours and the process was tiring, "It was an experience I won't forget, and I'm really glad I got to be a part of it."

Webster had similar comments. "This was not somewhere I normally go, but it was very interesting," she said in an interview Friday.

She said that McGee "found interesting activity that needs further study, and he will let us know how he interprets what we did."

Greeneville. Tenn.

Webster also said McGee wants to come back to the Dickson-Williams Mansion to finish "sweeping" the uppermost floor, and also wants to visit the historic stone "Greene County Gaol": a onetime county jail whose earliest section dates from 1882 but which uses some materials from a still-earlier jail located at the same site.

CHAPTER TWELVE

Tales of the
Gravedigger

Frank Thomas dug 8,000 graves but never buried a soul

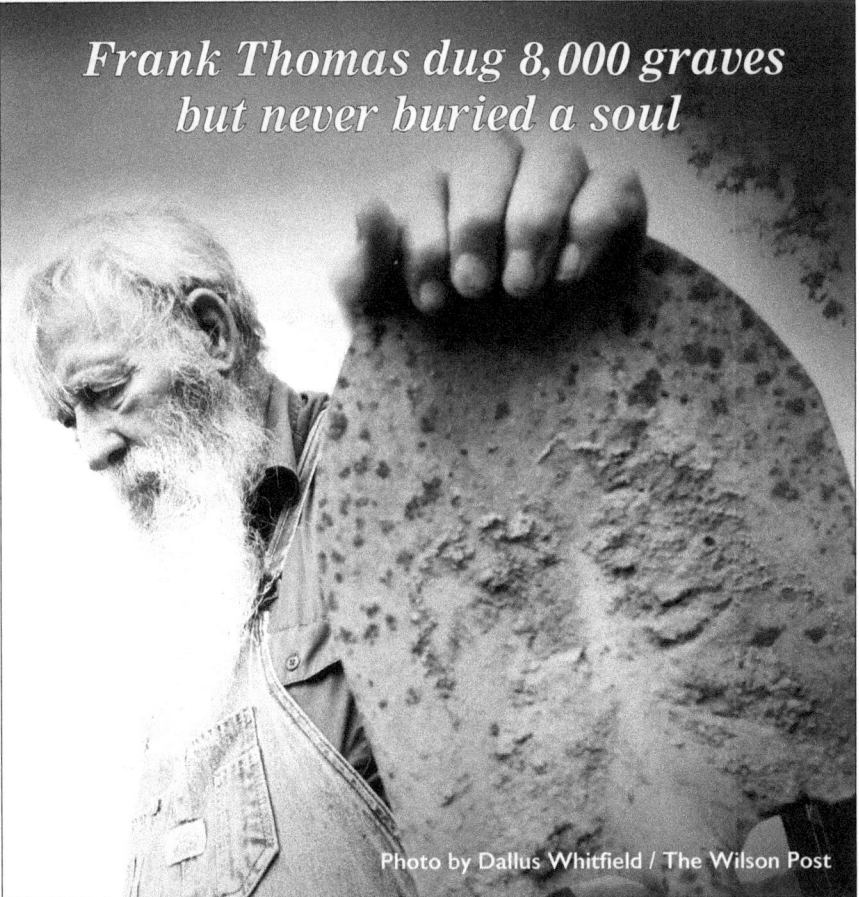

Photo by Dallus Whitfield / The Wilson Post

For the most part using a shovel, Frank Thomas dug thousands of graves during his lengthy career. He said, "You might think these fellows done this every day, your heart would harden, but my heart never hardened. I've cried at many a funeral and didn't even know the people."

67

Photo by Dallus Whitfield / The Wilson Post

Frank Thomas dug 8,000 graves in more than 30 counties over a 52-year career. He dug the majority of them by himself using a shovel and a pick. The 7-foot-tall retired gravedigger stands surrounded by tombstones in Salem Cemetery in Liberty, Tennessee. "For about 30 years, I buried almost everybody here," said Thomas, 78, who plans to be laid to rest in this graveyard.

Story by Ken Beck

The Wilson Post

LIBERTY, TENNESSEE — Few people have lowered more dead bodies down into the good Tennessee earth than gentle giant Frank Thomas.

Throughout his 45-year career, this 7-foot-tall Liberty native paid passionate attention to the details of carving out a perfect rectangle in the ground, a hole that would be the final resting place for a loved one.

"Anybody can dig a hole in the ground, but not anybody can dig a grave. It's a sacred place. I would say I've dug 8,000 graves. The first 35 years all by hand, most of the time me only," said Thomas, 78, who hung up his pick and shovel 12 years ago.

"I dug graves for all the funeral homes in DeKalb and Wilson County over the years. Sometimes I dug four a day, and they never did have to wait on me, but it was hard. I've dug a many a grave with a pick and shovel and didn't ever stop to get a drink of water, had my back bent until I finished, and then I'd go dig another."

> "Sometimes I dug four a day, and they never did have to wait on me, but it was hard. I've dug a many a grave with a pick and shovel and didn't ever stop to get a drink of water, had my back bent until I finished, and then I'd go dig another."

The gravedigger labored in hundreds of cemeteries across 37 Middle Tennessee counties.

"Cannon, Smith, Rutherford, Davidson, Williamson, White, Putnam, Bedford. I could just keep on naming them," he said, ticking off a partial list.

Among a handful of the businesses that requested his talents were Partlow, Ligon & Bobo and Nave funeral homes in Wilson County, Bass and Sanderson in Smith County, and Woodbury and Smith in Cannon County.

Wept over graves

Thomas tells on himself, saying, "You might think these fellows done this every day, your heart would harden, but my heart never hardened. I've cried at many a funeral and didn't even know the people. I always treated people, regardless of who they was, how poor they was, as nice and kind as I could be and showed 'em the respect they deserved.

"I been quit 12 years. When I first started, undertakers couldn't get nobody to dig graves. Nobody wanted to. They begged people to do it. When I began I didn't know nobody who dug graves as a profession. People looked down on me and acted like I was a low-class clown or trash, as if I couldn't find a living. But I saw I could make a good living at it. Now I know undertakers that has quit being undertakers to start digging graves."

> "Frank was probably one of the first ones that come in professionally, whether he meant to or not, and turned it into a business."

The gravedigger can spin tales of his calling for hours on end. He possesses a phenomenal memory, and if you gave him the name of one of the departed he laid to rest, he likely could tell you the cemetery where he or she reposes in the sleep of the ages.

Thomas has a few mementoes. "I've got dirt out of the first grave I ever dug in one bottle, and in another bottle is the dirt from the last grave. The first one was in Liberty and the last at Shop Springs in Bryan Cemetery," he recollected.

Thomas's final job was on Oct. 11, 2004, his 65th birthday.

"I sat there after everybody left and cried like a baby because I knew it was my last one. I enjoyed it. I didn't enjoy everybody dying. I won't get out of that myself," he said.

Started as teenager

Thomas began assisting a neighbor in digging graves for Evans Funeral Home in Liberty in the early 1950s. He was 13, and the chore allowed him to skip classes in high school. By the early

Photo by Dallus Whitfield / The Wilson Post
The dirt in these jars came from the first and the last graves that Frank Thomas helped dig. He began his 52-year career in 1952 and called it a day in 2004.

1960s, he had teamed with his father, Noble Thomas. At that time, the task paid a meager fee.

"Me and Daddy, we got $25 a grave, 12½ for him, 12½ for me. Mr. Jewell Nave [who operated funeral homes in Lebanon and Watertown] volunteered and gave me $35. Every year or two, I'd go up a little bit. Later on I had to furnish the lowering device, the tent, chairs and artificial turf. When I quit, I was getting $500. Now most are getting $800 or $900," he said.

"All that 45 years, I don't reckon but one grave I didn't have ready out of 8,000. It was solid rock, top to bottom. I take my work very, very seriously."

Thomas gave himself half a day to dig a grave if he didn't have a heavy load. If he were digging in soft soil clear of rock, he could cut it out in two hours or less. He was on call from fu-

> "I guess I went through 20 to 25 shovels. You wouldn't think a man would wear out a pick. Some of them I wore out to the nub."

neral home directors 24/7.

"Never had a vacation in my life. I can't think of but one or two Christmas days I spent with my wife and family," he said of digging across six decades.

He and his wife, Betty, have been married 54 years. He met her on the Woodbury town square, as she hails from the Cannon County community of Ivy Bluff. Betty is a quilter and stands 5-feet-tall to Frank's 7-feet. The couple raised a son and daughter and have four grandchildren.

They own a home in Liberty and a small farm in the DeKalb County countryside a few miles from where the Wilson, Cannon and DeKalb boundary lines meet.

Thomas also owns three acres of hallow ground on the back side of Salem Cemetery in Liberty where he sells burial plots. When his time comes, this is where he plans to be laid to rest.

Partner with his father

Born the son of a sharecropper, Thomas grew up with three brothers and graduated from Liberty High School in 1958. The sole survivor of his siblings, he dug two of their graves.

He says his father gave up farming to become a gravedigger.

"Daddy couldn't drive a vehicle. There were two other guys. One of them couldn't drive. The third guy had a pickup truck. They would dig graves for Walker Funeral Home in Smithville. That's where we all started," said Thomas.

"Then they started digging for two little funeral homes in Alexandria: Avant and Anderson. The old fellow who had the truck quit. After that the other guy quit, too. So that left Daddy without a job.

"Daddy said, 'I reckon I'll quit too.' I was working then as a bricklayer's helper. I said, 'No, Daddy, don't quit. I'll help.'"

A second funeral home in Smithville, Love-Cantrell, came calling, which allowed Frank and his father to work side by side in graveyards for six or seven years before the elder Thomas retired.

"I started it as my regular job in making a living in 1965. My son, Donald, started helping me when he was 8 years old and helped me in the summertime until he finished high school," said Thomas.

The myth of 6 feet under

Getting down to basics, he reported, "You've always heard a grave is 6 feet deep. That's not true. They're only 4½-feet deep, and 3-feet wide and 8-feet long. That is the standard around these parts. I always carried a 3-foot yardstick to make sure the grave is 3 feet wide, and I carried a 4-foot stick, flipped it twice to make sure it was long enough. I always wanted to be sure that the vault didn't hang [on its way down]."

"Now there are gravediggers that don't never get in the grave," said the man who carefully inspected the bottom of every grave he made.

"Back when I dug a grave by hand, you got to haul out about half the dirt. It would take 20 wheelbarrows full. Around the graveyard were peoples' graves that was sunk down, so I'd take that extra dirt and put it on those graves and take my rake and smooth it down. They don't do that now. They take a backhoe and take the dirt off behind the cemetery and dump it.

"I enjoyed it. The reason I enjoyed it so much is that most people, 95 percent of the families, were nice. Everyone treated me nice even though I was a nobody. After I got done, I'd go sit down on the back of the property and get out of the way till it comes my time to do things. There was a lot of times the family would go over and thank me for how I did it, not leaving a mess. Make me feel good. But it's not that way now."

Expanding boundaries

With his business firmly planted in DeKalb County, he then began getting calls from Wilson County funeral homes.

"Anybody can dig a hole in the ground, but not anybody can dig a grave. It's a sacred place."

"I was digging a grave one day in Alexandria at New Hope Cemetery. Mike Hunter [of Hunter Funeral Home in Watertown] drove up in front of the church, and he said, 'Can you dig a grave for us tomorrow?' I said, 'Why, yes, I reckon I can.'

"That body was coming out of Nashville, going to Jones Hill [cemetery]. I dug that one and next day had another to dig. Mr. Nave [Hunter's father-in-law, who owned Nave Funeral Home in Lebanon] called. I guess he buried 80 percent of the people in Wilson County.

"He had two men who dug graves. He said, 'If I call them, half the time they won't answer the phone.' He asked me, 'Will you dig my graves?' I said, 'It looks like I got a pretty heavy load, but yes, I will.'"

After preparing graves for Nave a couple of years, Ligon & Bobo Funeral called upon Thomas to do the same for them. And a few years later, Jackie Partlow, owner of Partlow Funeral Home, also requested his services.

"I remember one night, way after dark, Mr. Nave called and said, 'Frank, I've got one to bury in Greenvale.' I had another

On rare occasion, Frank Thomas dug as many as five graves in a day. "Them's two hardworking hands. I guarantee you that," he said.

grave to dig the next day over in Jackson County.

"About midnight I got out of bed and told my wife, 'I'm going to dig that grave.' I carried a coal oil lamp and got up there with that lamp and went over that graveyard hunting that tombstone, and I lit into it. When undertakers set the time for a funeral, they're not gonna change it. I had as high as a five graves a day. I really had to move dirt to get 'em dug.

"Seventy-five percent of the time I was digging, they would bury 'em that day. I'd get up by daylight, drive my car to the cemetery and look for the tombstone with a cigarette lighter."

Neither snow nor rain nor heat

Just like a farmer, the gravedigger found that his work in terra firma could turn into torment caused due to extreme weather and rocky ground.

"It didn't matter how hot or how cold it was. I even dug one

75

in a tornado. It come a tornado, blowed my tent plumb down. So much water turned into the grave, we had to wait two or three hours to bury the body," he said.

"One year we had an inch of ice and six inches of snow on the ground, and me and my boy was asked to bury a lady on Jones Hill. It was coldest day on record for that day, 18 degrees below zero. The grave was at the back end, and me and my boy put all our stuff in a little red wagon and pulled it up that hill like a mule. While we were in the grave, icicles formed on our caps. Later that afternoon, they salted the road for the folks coming to the funeral."

So what did the gravedigger do when his shovel struck limestone?

"We'd take a sledgehammer and bust our brains out," answered Thomas. "If we couldn't get it, we'd call back to the funeral home and have them call a contactor to drill or dynamite it.

"People out of McMinnville came out with a grave-digging machine in the mid-1970s. Awfullest-looking thing you ever seen but dug prettiest graves you ever seen. So I go to buy me one, a little ole Terrmite backhoe that had a 14-horsepower Briggs & Stratton engine, and I hated that thing. I'd take it to the graveyard a many a time and leave it on the driveway and dig the grave by hand. So I sold that thing."

Thomas's tools of the trade were his trusty shovel and pick. He also carried an ax to cut out tree roots, a claw hammer to nail down the top of wood coffins and a hand broom to sweep the bottom of the grave clean.

"We'd take a sledgehammer and bust our brains out," answered Thomas. "If we couldn't get it, we'd call back to the funeral home and have them call a contactor to drill or dynamite it."

"I guess I went through 20 to 25 shovels. You wouldn't think a man would wear out a pick. Some of them I wore out to the nub," he said.

Ghost in the cemetery?

While not a man who believes in haunts, he confessed that he was spooked so badly one night that he fled a graveyard.

"The scariest thing, I'm digging one at Horton Springs in Smith County, one of the times had to get it done that day. I was digging by hand at night in the bottom by truck light. Them lights was shining on tombstones. All of a sudden I heard a woman hollering. I raised up and looked around the graveyard. I didn't see a soul.

"She hollered again. I loaded my stuff and shovel in the back and got in my truck and went home. I came back next morning to finish it. I never saw nobody," he said with a laugh.

CHAPTER THIRTEEN

Part 2: Tales of the Gravedigger

Photo by Dallus Whitfield / The Wilson Post

"I sat there after everybody left and cried like a baby because I knew it was my last one. I enjoyed it. I didn't enjoy everybody dying. I won't get out of that myself."

Story by Ken Beck
The Wilson Post

A bit more than halfway through his 50-plus-year career, gravedigger Frank Thomas hired two young men, Michael Hunter and Kenneth Vickers, to help him on occasion.

He has never forgotten the time they scoffed after he told them about hand digging a grave in an hour and 45 minutes. Months later, the two went to the same Mt. Juliet cemetery to dig a grave, and a man, who lived nearby, strolled over to tell them about the tall man he observed digging a grave in an hour and 15 minutes.

Thomas said, "Michael helped me all through high school. After college, he came back home and wanted to know if he could work with me. He was with me over 20 years off and on. One of the best hands I ever had, he and my boy."

Hunter and Vickers later worked as a gravedigging team for four or five years. Hunter started his own Hunter Grave Service (HGS) 10 years ago, and he now prepares about 200 graves a year.

Protégé shares observations

Hunter, 50, began helping Thomas when he was 18. At the time the veteran had been digging graves for his grandfather, Mr. Jewell Nave, and father, Mike Hunter, for more than 15 years.

Said Hunter, "Frank got everybody for my granddaddy from the 1960s until my granddaddy died in 1997, unless they [the bodies] went to Wilson County Memorial Garden or Cedar Grove. And the last 20 or so years he worked, Frank dug in Cedar Grove.

"Frank was probably one of the first ones that come in professionally, whether he meant to or not, and turned it into a business. I remember Frank telling me the first time he was hand-picking a grave up at New Hope Cemetery, my daddy drove up and got out his car and said, 'I've got a grave at Jones Hill. You want to dig it for me?' He never said no to anybody.

"From that time on he dug every grave for my daddy. About a week after that, my granddaddy called up at Liberty and said, 'This is Jewell Nave. You opened a grave for Mike up at Watertown, and I wondered if you would come up to Lebanon and dig a grave for me?' And from that point on, my granddaddy used him every grave after that."

Michael Hunter helps Frank Thomas as he digs a grave.

'Last of a dying breed'

"When I went to work with him in 1984, he was practically digging everything in Wilson County and DeKalb, and since Frank retired, there's probably six, maybe eight sets of gravediggers that do what he used to do by himself. That is how gravedigging kind of evolved. It ain't that long since the communities went out and dug the graves," said Hunter.

"He's the last of a dying breed. I don't think nobody's gonna dig that many graves by hand again. He was the transition between the families or communities that came out and dug a grave and to when it turned into a business. He was the one around here. Won't never be anybody else like him.

"I remember back in the '80s, when I first started helping Frank. We would go to most of these country cemeteries in Wilson County. One of them I think of right off hand is Conatser Cemetery off Berea Church Road off Coles Ferry Pike. We would go the day before to dig and go back the next day and do the funeral service.

"There would always be five or six old men show up, and they would watch us work. They would start telling the stories of how they used to hand dig the graves. Some of them would tell WWII stories and all that kind of stuff. They have slowly all passed away, and when we go to these cemeteries today, nobody shows up like that.

"From my perspective, those guys took an active part in digging graves during their lives, and Frank was the first to take it on to the business route. There's people that work at cemeteries, and there's gravediggers. There's a big difference between them. There's not many true gravediggers. There's more now than when Frank did it solo, but still, as a profession, there are not that many gravediggers.

Keeping traditions alive

"A gravedigger deals mainly in these country church cemeteries, community cemeteries and family cemeteries. That's where we primarily make our living. They don't have cemetery workers there to do the work," said Hunter.

Photo by Dallus Whitfield / The Wilson Post

"You've got your corporate cemeteries, like Wilson County Memorial Garden. They hire people to work at the cemetery. In Nashville most of your cemeteries are corporate. You go to Memorial Garden, they're gonna back a tractor down a row of graves and have a hydraulic dump trailer behind it, and they're gonna dump that grave full of dirt instead of hand filling in.

"You would almost have to see it to truly know what I am talking about. There's a difference between what we do, but it is the same job.

"Frank would always quit digging out of the grave a little bit early and finish the rest of the grave with a pick and a trim bar. We would shovel it out, and the bottom would be perfectly flat, even to the corners, and today most don't even get into the grave.

"I make my graves 100 percent to specifications because I learned trimming graves from Frank. I've kept the 4-foot and 3-foot yardsticks when the majority of gravediggers use a tape measure now," said Hunter, who does the brunt of the digging with a mini-excavator and busts up rock with a 500-pound jack-hammer.

"Frank was one of first that cut the sod up and hand rolled it. Most people think we use a machine to take it up. It's a little more work but a lot of people really like that. Most people have gone to hydraulic dump cart or a ratchet cart. To me it's just as easy to calculate your dirt, put it on a cart and shovel it in. Families still like that, what I call the traditional way.

"I never remember Frank ever making a mistake in the cemetery, and I've tried to apply that to this day, and I've never had a problem. He loved helping the people in their time of need and people remember that. You just don't see that personal touch any more, and Frank brought that. I try to keep that part of it alive and well."

On the lighter side, Hunter hints at Thomas's sense of humor and his stamina, saying, "One time he paid me off in Susan B. Anthony dollars, and he was always threatening that he was going to pay me with pennies.

"Frank is pretty stout. He wouldn't stop. It wouldn't be fast work but a steady pace all day.

He never did beat me in arm wrestling but will tell you that I never beat him.

"I considered him one of my best friends, and I learned a lot from him. I tell him when I go to the cemetery, he's with me. He knows every grave that he has dug," said the student about his master.

Politician with a slogan

The gravedigger was not all work and no play. He enjoyed a long stretch as a local politician, as he four times was elected a DeKalb County Commissioner. He said, "I ran against a banker and a preacher, and the gravedigger won."

A souvenir from his politicking days survives in his packed garage. It reads:

Elect Frank Thomas

County Commissioner

Second District

The Last One To Let You Down

During his leisure time, Thomas attends to nine horses on his farm. He owns two new and three used buggies and enjoys hitching up a horse to his favorite buggy and going out for a spin.

"One of the things I love the best of all is going to Watertown for a haircut at Barrett's on the square. On purpose I turned one buggy into being the junkiest-looking thing for the fun of it. I like the attention. People will stop their cars and try to give me money," he said with a grin.

He also got a kick out digging a grave for a Ray Stevens music video and portraying a bum for a scene in the 2008 feature film, "Billy: The Early Years," about evangelist Billy Graham," which was shot at the Wilson County Fairground.

Portrait in wood

Since retirement, he has turned an artistic hand toward making walking sticks. He has turned a few of the 150 or more he has crafted into memorials in honor of people who have died in the community and given them to their families as keepsakes.

During conversation in his farmhouse, Thomas pulls out a hunk of wood and flips it over to show a painted carving of a tall man holding a shovel and standing on a pile of dirt.

He said, "There's the gravedigger himself. That's me."

Thomas explained that a close friend, the late Jimmy Smith of Liberty, carved and painted the piece for him in 2004. Smith died not long afterward. At his funeral, after the preacher finished

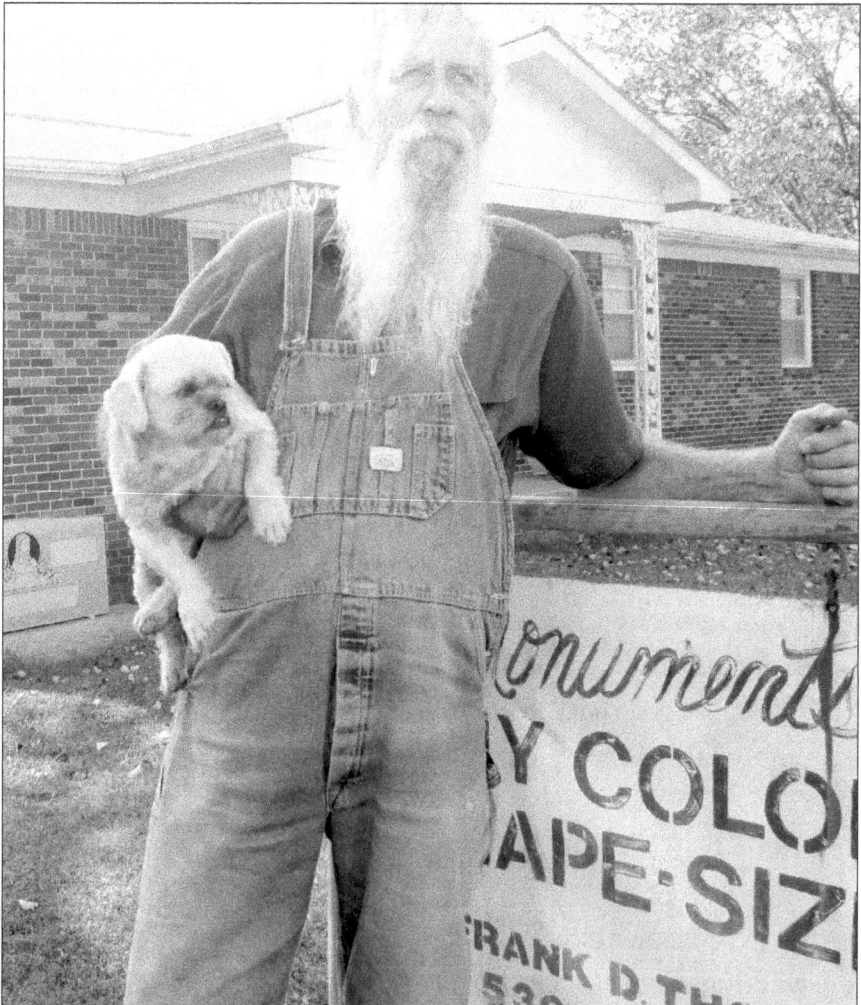

Photo by Dallus Whitfield / The Wilson Post

The retired Liberty gravedigger today sells monuments of any color, shape or size and has samples of tombstones in his front yard. He poses here with his dog, Sam, 8, and says, "Sam is my best friend ever, non-human. I'm gonna have him buried right beside me."

speaking, Thomas stood before the mourners and spoke a few words about his friendship with Smith and showed the crowd his carving. That was the only time in 8,000 funerals that Thomas spoke his piece.

Poetry on a tombstone

In the early 1990s, Thomas started a side business of peddling tombstones. Samples sit in plain view in his front yard off Highway 70.

After selling one grave marker, he recalled, the customer said he wanted some sort of verse cut on the stone.

"He asked me, 'What should I put?' I said, 'What about putting three words on there? 'Love never dies.' That about tickled them to death. All but one [customer] have done that," said Thomas, mighty pleased of his slogan.

"There was a time during the last few years I dug when I had two broken legs. I had to go to the graveyard in a walker straight from the hospital to show the boys where to dig. I had a stroke, had cancer. It was rough. Most people was nice that I dealt with. I never contraried nobody," he said.

Asked if he knew who would dig his grave, the thoughtful gravedigger responded, "I have thought about digging it myself and digging it by hand. I'd have to keep it covered. If anything happens and I don't dig it, Michael will be the one that digs it."

Presence still requested

"I enjoyed my work, made a good living, raised a family, built a new house, bought this little ole farm. I reckon I'm the first person in these parts of the country to make a living as a grave-digger."

Even now, 12 years since he ceased digging, folks request his presence at funerals, from beginning to the very end.

"People call me now to see their graves dug and some want me to let the casket down, and some want me to throw the first dirt in. Then they tell me, 'When we die, if you're still living, we want you to do the same for us.'"

Taking pride in his lengthy, mostly solitary career, Thomas has these words emblazoned on the back window of his white, 2002 Chevy pickup: Retired Gravedigger. I Dug Graves For 45 Years But Never Did I Bury One Soul."

Interpreting the meaning, he says, "I tell people, 'I buried the body. The Good Lord takes care of the soul.'"

CHAPTER FOURTEEN

The
Spiritual Realm

*Understanding a gift beginning
at four years of age*

By Linda Braden Albert

The Daily Times, Maryville

Randy DeLong was about 4 years old when he met the older couple he came to consider as another set of grandparents. They lived in his house, spoke with German accents and taught him words of their native tongue.

> What we have found is that we carry our personalities into the afterlife. So if you have an old curmudgeon that lived kind of mean when he was here, you're going to have the same old curmudgeon.

Only DeLong could see them, hear them, interact with them — they were spirits.

"Every house we moved to after that had a presence in the house," DeLong recalled. "I grew up comforted by them. They never frightened me."

His mother helped him accept the gift of sensing the spirits and ghosts around him, but as he grew into an adult, the world had different ideas and he tried to fit in with those.

DeLong said, "I thought maybe I was just odd, but as I got older, I figured it just didn't matter."

DeLong met and married his wife, Doris, who has the same gifts as far as sensing paranormal activity, and later moved to Blount County. The rich history of this area was so intriguing that they began exploring some of the lesser known areas of the county.

"It has a level of paranormal activity not found in most areas of the country," DeLong said. "So began Maryville Old-school Paranormal Society, or M.O.P.S., in 2009.

We wanted to share the history of the area from a new perspective and bring the spirit realm into the light."

Misconceptions

People fear what they don't understand, and paranormal activity is definitely one of those subjects. DeLong said the misconceptions come from television shows and movies that play up the darker side. In his experience, however, "99.9 percent of it is just a relative or a passing spirit."

He said many of the calls he and Doris receive are from people who think they have something evil, or a demon, in their homes.

"I've been doing this a lot of years and I've never run into anything evil, personally. What we have found is that we carry our personalities into the afterlife. So if you have an old curmudgeon that lived kind of mean when he was here, you're going to have the same old curmudgeon. But I've never run into anything dangerous or true evil. I'm not saying it's not out there, but I've never run into it. ... There's not a demon in every attic."

Tools of the trade

The DeLongs use the "old-school" equipment for their investigations — a Sanyo digital camera, a Sony handicam, a Ghostbox, a digital recorder and their own sensitivity to the spirits around them. DeLong explained how the equipment is used.

"If you take a digital recorder into an active area and you're recording, sometimes you will pick up spirit voices, called an electronic voice phenomenon (EVP)," he said. "We use the Ghostbox with the digital recorder. A Ghostbox is simply an AM/FM radio that's been modified to scan the frequencies really quickly, and it gives spirits raw audio that they can use to speak. It gives you instantaneous responses to questions. You can almost carry on a great detailed conversation."

The Smoky Mountains and Cades Cove, in particular, are

favorite places for the ghost hunters to explore. DeLong said, "When you take the time to slow down and listen, you will feel the energy of the people around you."

The Thompson-Brown House/Cades Cove Museum on Lamar Alexander Parkway in Maryville is another site burgeoning with spirit activity. The house was built in the early 19th century, plus it houses artifacts from families who once lived in Cades Cove. Museum curator Gloria Motter often has her hair tugged, her shoulder touched. She told DeLong recently she sensed a new presence in the old house.

"Somebody's been lying on the bed, and we've been trying to get answers on who's passing through," DeLong said.

"Help me"

DeLong said he and Doris search for answers because they don't really know why spirits and ghosts continue to stay on the Earth.

> "There are so many question, and the answers are so hard to come by," he said. "We haven't gotten answers so we keep asking different questions. We don't know if they aren't allowed to answer

"There are so many question, and the answers are so hard to come by," he said. "We haven't gotten answers so we keep asking different questions. We don't know if they aren't allowed to answer ... None of us are ever really going to know until we are the answer. We can only speculate, theorize."

In the course of the investigations, an EVP may answer, "Help" or "Help me."

"It just boggles my mind when investigators go in and they get 'Help me' as answers from EVPs, and they don't help," DeLong said. "That's when you keep going back and asking, 'What do you need help with?'"

He explained the distinction between a ghost and a spirit.

"A ghost is somebody that doesn't know that they've passed," he said. "A spirit has gone into the light, knows what Heaven is, knows God, but has come back and is, like, watching over somebody. So when we come across something, we ask them if they have seen the light. If you get the word 'no' and they seem confused, we ask them to look for a light, imagine a light, let the light get bigger, and keep talking and talking about the light. We tell them to let us know when they cross into the light, that they will have friends and relatives there waiting.

Nine out of 10 times you'll get a sound in the house or you'll get a feeling they've crossed into that light. That doesn't mean they don't come back, but at least they get their answers — we're hoping. Again, we don't know, but it feels more comfortable.

"A lot of groups do what they call 'cleansing' of houses, and they think they're getting rid of the spirit. I don't think you ever get rid of a spirit. You'll tone down the energy, but we've noticed that the spirit stays where it's at. It's comfortable. That's like somebody coming into your house and asking you to leave. Well, you're not going to leave, it's your house, but you may tone yourself down a little bit.

How would you like to be treated?

"They are people. How would you like to be treated? We always ask if we can come in. You can carry on a conversation just like you would if you're meeting somebody and going into their house. That's where we get great evidence, just sitting down and talking."

DeLong now has end-stage emphysema. His health no longer allows him to investigate private residences, but he and Doris

93

still explore this area. They advise other groups on their methods of recording evidence and how to investigate with the utmost respect for the spirits. DeLong said, "In our short time as a group, we have helped hundreds of people understand that what goes bump in the night isn't as scary as what you might think."

CHAPTER FIFTEEN

The
Downtown
Prankster

*Meet "Otis," who haunts
the Shoppes of Marketplace*

Photo by Mike Williams
Does "Otis" peer out from the windows above the Shoppes of Marketplace, observing the
citizens of Rogersville?

By Rebekah Wilson

The Rogersville Review

"I'll believe it when I see it," may be wise words to live by, but the employees of The Looking Glass and Compuserve have seen and do, in fact, believe.

Fondly named "Otis" by Anne Dewitte of The Looking Glass, the ghost that haunts the Shoppes of Marketplace is well known for making mischief at both The Looking Glass and Compuserve.

However, Rogersville Historian Henry Price gave the employees reason to believe that the ghost might respond in a friendlier manner to the name Tom, or Thomas Galloway Brownlow.

Brownlow, who was a tinsmith, built the Brownlow Hotel, where the two businesses are now located, in the 1860s. "Brownlow loved gears and gadgets. He built what looked like an old Goldberg Machine in his tin shop," Price said. "Children would stop and stare through the window."

However, when Brownlow died, the gears didn't stop turning, said Price. "I have heard that when people would pass by the old hotel in the dark, they could still hear the gears."

Brownlow's love for gears can explain some of the strange happenings in the old hotel building.

Scott McNabb of Compuserve said objects often disappear from the office. "We wind up missing tools and CDs sometimes. Occasionally I will jokingly say 'Otis, bring that back!' and it will show up soon after."

"Otis" also likes to play with the fluorescent sign in the window of Compuserve, said Mark Dewitte.

"I'll turn off the light and go home, and when I drive back by the store, the lights will be back on," he said.

Some of the hauntings at The Looking Glass have involved curling irons, noted Gena Reynolds.

"We turn the curling irons off before we leave. We make sure

A ghost is said to linger in and around the former location of The Looking Glass and other downtown businesses. — File photo.

of it. And when we come in the next morning, they will all be turned on," she said.

Reynolds also told a story about the lights. A former employee of Compuserve came in The Looking Glass to use the rest room when the lights were off. "He said 'Gosh, I wish the lights would come on,' and the lights came on."

Though "Otis" seems to be a prankster, always moving objects and playing with lights, sometimes he seems to be just passing through, said McNabb.

"I was in here by myself one time, and the back door opened and closed," he said. "I got up to see who it was, and no one was there. Then, the front door opened and closed and the glass door opened and closed. It was as if he was just walking by," McNabb said.

When the subject of ghosts arises, most people skeptically try to find other explanations for the odd occurrences. However, McNabb and Anne Dewitte have seen "Otis."

The apparition appeared to McNabb one night after Compuserve installed the doorbell. "The bell rang once as if someone came in and again as if someone left," he said. "I got up and couldn't see anyone, but I could see Anne's mirror across the hall, and I saw him in the mirror."

Both McNabb and Anne Dewitte describe the apparition as a gray, smoky figure.

Anne, however, has seen the figure more than once. The strangest encounter with "Otis" at The Looking Glass involved Reynolds' daughter, Autumn.

"I was up front doing hair," Anne said, "and I saw something go by, but I didn't say anything because the shop was busy.

"Reynolds' daughter, Autumn, went back to the bathroom and called for me. I went back and asked her what she wanted and she said, 'Don't worry. I see it too.'"

No matter how bone-chilling and creepy these stories may be, nothing devastating or hurtful has ever resulted from the spook that resides in the Shoppes of Marketplace.

"They are just pranks," said Dewitte of Compuserve. "Nothing harmful has ever happened."

Whether the ghost is truly Thomas Galloway Brownlow or just plain "Otis," the employees of The Looking Glass and Compuserve have stopped trying to explain the strange occurrences and have learned to share their businesses with this prankster from beyond.

This story originally appeared in the September 11, 2002 edition of The Rogersville Review. The Looking Glass and Compuserve have since moved from this location.

CHAPTER SIXTEEN

Ghost Busters

*Paranormal investigators
have spirit for the hunt*

Robert Norris

The Daily Times, Maryville

"OK, we've got cameras running, people. Kill the lights."

The voice belongs to Jason La Follette, a Blount Countian and chairman of the Southeastern Paranormal Research Society (SEPRS).

> "We've been working late at night and you'll hear that door close. Well, it's on a spring. The wind can't catch it. It won't move. Same thing with the curtains. The curtains are always closed, but sometimes when you hear the door close you'll come over and the curtains are open."

But his voice isn't what he and five other paranormal investigators are listening for late Wednesday night at a six-decade-old building on East Broadway Avenue in Maryville.

They are looking for evidence of paranormal happenings -- in layman's language, ghosts.

The building was home to Drake Auto Parts for many years. Now it houses Southland Books, Detour Coffee and Southern Studios Stained Glass.

Lisa Misosky owns the bookstore, and loves the old building, but she's not so comfortable with the odd occurrences that seem to happen only at night.

She suspects the covered spring under the building may have something to do with that.

"From what we understand, moving water is an attraction for ..." Misosky, pauses searching for the right word. "For energy, I guess."

Energy that does what? The black screen door in the back of the building is an example.

'Hear door close'

"We've been working late at night and you'll hear that door close. Well, it's on a spring. The wind can't catch it. It won't move. Same thing with the curtains. The curtains are always closed, but sometimes when you hear the door close you'll come over and the curtains are open," Misosky says.

"It's kind of disturbing when you're alone in the store."

Valerie Spence, owner of the coffee shop, says she's heard the screen door close and unexplained sounds coming from the far corner of the stained-glass studio.

She also wonders about the impact of the spring that was filled in when the building was constructed.

"I don't know, it just seems like a natural phenomenon, like that might have some sort of repercussions -- but nothing scary. I've never been frightened."

La Follette has an explanation.

"It's kicking extra energy into the air, and paranormal off of that," he says.

"I've seen that on TAPS," Spence says, referring to The Atlantic Paranormal Society paranormal investigators on the *Ghost Hunters* TV show.

Later, there's no tapping as the SPRS ghost hunters monitor the images on the laptop and move up and down the isles of the

bookstore. Lanes labeled Classics & Literature, Thriller, Histori-cal Romance, Modern Novel, Horror, Mystery, Sci-Fi & Fantasy and an interesting subgenre, Paranormal Romance with titles like *Dead and Loving It* and *Kiss Me Forever*.

What was that?

One camera shows flick-ers of light.

"What was that?"

"Some kind of mist or something," says Eddie Robinson, lead investigator.

One of the investigators announces he's detected something.

"Had a cold spot in the back corner about 10 de-grees below ambient tem-perature."

That's the far corner of the stained-glass shop, same place where Spence heard sounds coming from.

And there's a voice. But this one is identifiable. One of the investigators is lying on a couch in the middle of the darkened store, trying to summon spirits.

"I'm waiting for a sign. Are you male or female? We came all the way out here to talk to you; give us a sign."

Alas, there's nothing definitive. Some flashes of light on the monitor that could just be dust.

The EVP, the electronic voice phenomena device, squawks some sounds resembling words but in random patterns. It's an-noying, and is turned off.

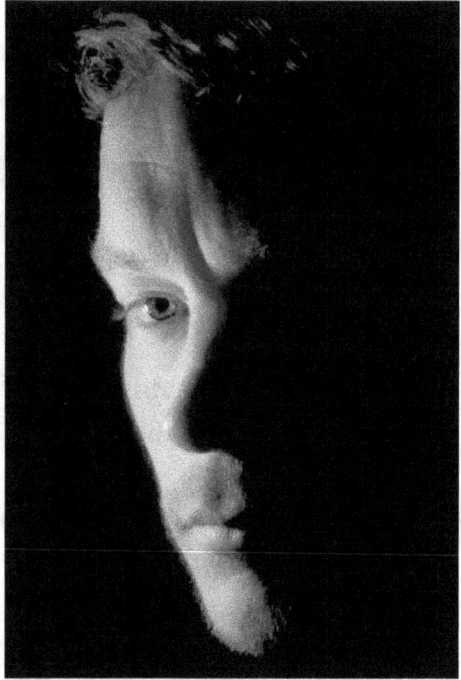

Stakeout for ghosts

That's normal, La Follette says. Like detectives on a crime stakeout, it's mostly waiting.

"A stakeout for ghosts, I guess that's what this is," he says.

In the early hours of Thursday morning, the group calls it quits for the night's investigation.

Maybe the only ghosts at the bookstore are ghost writers haunting the Film Biographies section -- the place where the actual authors of movie stars' "autobiographies" find their names missing from their works.

After getting some sleep, La Follette picks up the investigation the next day by reviewing images captured on the computer's hard drive. He's found something. Reproductions from the infrared cameras that show a hazy, circular-shaped spot in one of the bookstore's isles -- an "orb."

"Here's the three pictures. The only difference between the original files and the copy files is the addition on the arrow. Unlike dust which moves through the frame, this appears, solidifies in the same position, and then disappears in the same position. This happens over three frames which is a total of 3/10th of a second," La Follette says.

"This could be significant because it is by the records in the back right corner of the store, where we got the moving cold spot last night. Of course, it could be nothing," he adds.

"Honestly, with no more evidence that one cold spot and one 'orb,' it would be a little premature for us to pronounce the bookstore haunted. However, with these two pieces of evidence, it would certainly be a place for us to take a second look one night."

For information about the Southeastern Paranormal Research Society, check the Web at www.seprs.net.

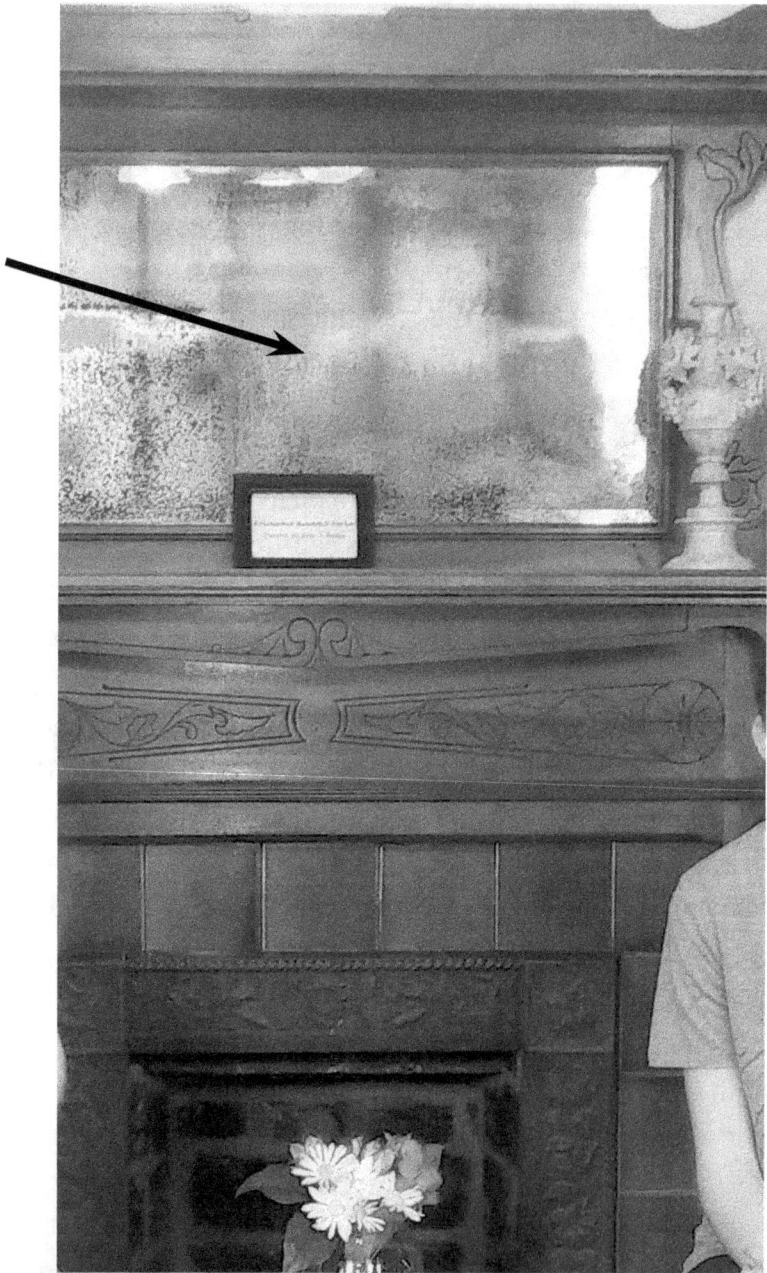

This photo by Knoxville author Janena White shows what
appears to be an image in the mirror behind her daughter.
Janena didn't notice the figure while taking the photo, but
recognized it later. Taken in Historic Westwood House in
Knoxville, Tennessee August 2017.

CHAPTER SEVENTEEN

The Blue Hole

"As I turn, I catch a glimpse, just for an instant, of a white figure."

Story by Angie Gambill
The Tomahawk, Mountain City

As I wind my way down the little road through the Walnut Grove Community, specks of bright morning sunshine dance in the fields encircling me. A shower of scarlet, amber and copper leaves fall to the ground in a swirl of color. My eyes are drawn upward to powder puff clouds set against an azure sky, and childhood memories bring a smile to my heart. The smoldering embers of my love for the autumn season, the sunset of summer, are rekindled and come to a full roaring blaze inside me.

Then a sudden chill sends a shiver through me and I physically shudder as I round the bend leading to the old rock quarry. The fiery colors of fall, so overwhelming only yards up the road, have faded to dingy brown remnants of summer lying in damp

Picture by Lacy Hilliard

piles in the road before me. Overhead, the sun shines as brightly and majestically as ever, but somehow neither its light nor its warmth penetrates into the gloomy world I have entered. Peering through the chain link fence surrounding "The Blue Hole" to the dark, murky waters beyond, the origin of its name escapes me momentarily. Surely no hint of such a rich and vibrant hue has ever graced this dismal place. It would more aptly be called "The Hole of Shadows" or "The Miry Depths."

Not a hint remains of the youthful and light-hearted Mary that stepped into the depths so long ago. I search in vain for a glimpse of the ivory tones of her alabaster skin. Is there no token of her ruby red lips or the rosy blush the fever left on her cheeks? Even the shiny raven shades of her long silky hair have surely been washed away by this somber place. Her flowing white night-gown must be as drab and gray as the waters that closed over her head.

A sea captain and his wife and their only daughter, Mary, had come to the mountains of Tennessee for a change of scenery from their cottage on the seacoast of Charleston. The old two-story house they stayed in just up the road from the quarry was drafty and cold, and the chilly mountain night air quickly took its toll on Mary. She longed for the ocean and the warm, salty breezes that had been her very breath since birth. At night as she lay in her bed, she strained to hear the gulls calling to each other, but was rewarded only with the sound of a cold wind moaning through the boughs of the oak tree outside her room.

Mary's parents watched her, day after day, night after night, as she grew paler and weaker and more and more withdrawn from those that loved her. They contacted doctors and specialists who frantically searched for a cure to the mysterious ailment that was draining the life from Mary right before their eyes.

Mary's only solace came when she visited the pond that had formed in the recesses of the rock quarry down the lane. She would lie on the bank for hours, eyes closed, listening to the lapping of the waves against the rocks at the water's edge. She imagined she was back home in Charleston, warm and safe and happy again.

Despite Mary's trips to the quarry and the doctors' best efforts, her condition continued to deteriorate. By autumn she had developed a high fever that sometimes left her weak and lifeless but more often wild and uncontrollable in her delirium.

During one such manic day in late October, Mary's mother, exhausted from the constant care her daughter required, fell sound asleep at her bedside just as darkness crept across the floors of her room. A few short hours later, she woke with a start to find Mary's bed dampened from the fever's perspiration, but empty. Mary was not to be found. She woke her husband and together they frantically searched the house for the fever-crazed girl, but to no avail.

As her parents moved their search outdoors, they hurried to Mary's special place at the rock quarry, and much to their horror, saw the pale form of their daughter hovering at the water's edge. Their panicked cries to her as they ran the short distance to the pond brought no response, as she slowly, almost methodically, stepped into the water. Mary continued her walk into the depths of The Blue Hole, never hesitating, never shifting her gaze from whatever vision lay before her. Her parents reached the water just as the murky liquid closed over her head. Again and again, Mary's father dove into the frigid water, but to no avail. The blackness had quickly and completely swallowed the delirious girl. In the days that followed, countless attempts to recover the body were made, but Mary was gone.

At long last, Mary had found her way home. Home to her sandy beaches and sea air. Home to her seagulls and warm breezes.

Turning from the gloom of the murky waters before me, I suddenly feel an urgent need for the warmth and sunshine of the road that brought me here. Behind me, the air stirs, and a pungent scent of salt air sweeps over me. As I turn, I catch a glimpse, just for an instant, of a white figure, gliding ever so slowly above the surface of the black liquid of The Blue Hole. I see her shining black hair falling in cascades over her pale shoulders and her long white nightgown flowing in the breeze. As her lips part, I sense more than hear, a single word floating on the ocean breeze. "Home."

At that moment, I knew the origin of its name. I knew why this place so devoid of life and color is known as "The Blue Hole." One look into the sapphire blue eyes of Mary, and all the drab and dingy shadows melted away.

CHAPTER EIGHTEEN

Murder in
Dr. Baker's House

*The Murder of Doctor Harvey Baker
by the Yankees*

Knoxville Daily Register
June 23, 1863

We have learned of all particulars of this cold-blooded and in-human murder of one of our most estimable citizens by the East Tennessee Tories and their allies, the Yankees.

Dr. Baker's house is about ten miles below Knoxville, on the main Western road. On Friday afternoon last he told his wife and family he could do no good staying at home, and believed he would come up to town where he might be of some assistance in its defense. He got his gun and was in his yard when a Yankee rode up and presented his gun at him. Dr. B told him not to shoot, that he was a citizen and did not belong to the army. But the soldier in place of desisting raised his gun to his face to take sight and fired, Dr. B firing at about the same time. Dr. B then went into his house and locked the doors, sending his family upstairs. His wife insisted he should go up stairs with them, which he did soon after.

> The Yankees present having exhausted their ammunition threw their guns with fixed bayonets, at him – he throwing the guns back again at them.

In a short time the soldier who had fired on Dr. Baker brought up a large number of men who surrounded the house and commenced firing through the windows on both sides, demanding that the men in the house should surrender.

Mrs. Baker came to the window and told them there was no man in the house but her husband, and if they would cease firing he would surrender – they continued firing, and Dr. Baker came to the window once or twice, and told them, there was no man in the house but himself, and if they would cease firing, he would surrender. But whenever he presented himself at the window, they fired on him, and he returned the fire with his pistol. In a few minutes a number of them broke open the lower doors and entered the house, and commenced firing though the ceiling into the room where Dr. Baker and his family were.

They then went up the stairway and demanded that the men should come out and surrender. Mrs. Baker came out and told them there was no man in the house except Dr. Baker, and if they would not fire upon him he would come out. They ordered her to go away from the door or they would shoot her. Dr. Baker then pulled his wife in the room and threw the doors open! They fired upon him with their guns and he returned the fire with his pistols.

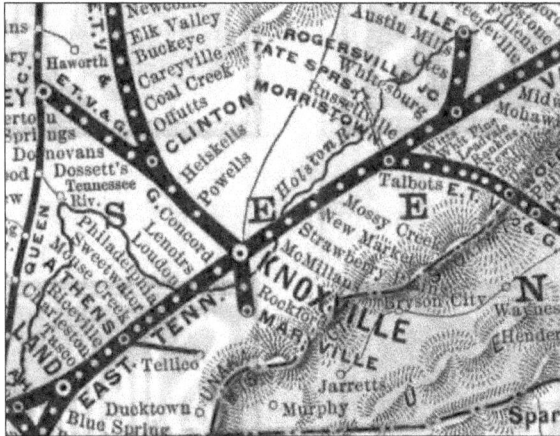

The Yankees present having exhausted their ammunition threw their guns with fixed bayonets, at him – he throwing the guns back again at them. A number of Yankee reinforcements then came up with loaded guns and fired a volley at him, inflicting two mortal wounds. Dr. Baker said to his wife, "They have killed me," and fell; his wife, in endeavoring to support him, fell with him. The Yankees then entered the room – one of them who had no bayonet on his gun, jabbed him in the mouth with the muzzle of his gun – another run his bayonet through his cheek – others struck him in the head – one ruffian pushed Mrs. Baker aside from her husband with his bayonet.

Dr. Baker asked to be turned on his side, and asked for water. After he drank, he observed the crowd of Yankees around him that they were a cowardly set of scoundrels, so many of them to assault and murder one man.

Two of the Yankees were dangerously if not mortally wounded. They went to the next house and had their wounds dressed, and said Dr. Baker was the gamest man they ever saw.

Dr. Baker was one of the earliest of our citizens to espouse the cause of the South, and was an ardent secessionist from the beginning. We have no doubt some renegade Tory from East Tennessee had given the Yankees full information about Dr. Baker's sentiments and his activity in the cause of the South, and that they intended to seize upon some pretense to murder him.

After the cowardly scoundrels had murdered her husband, they commenced robbing his wife of her jewelry and carried off everything they could find of value that was easy to be concealed. Among other things, they took a breast pin containing a miniature likeness of Dr. Baker set in gold.

CHAPTER NINETEEN

The
Ghost Upstairs

Hauntings at the Baker-Peters House

By Wendy Smith
Knoxville News Sentinel -
Shopper News

Confederate soldier Abner
Baker came home from the
war looking for trouble, and he
found it. According to those who
frequent his former home, the
Baker-Peters house at the cor-
ner of Peters Road and Kingston Pike, Abner continues to make
mischief today.

Abner Baker was the son of Dr. Harvey Baker, who built the
antebellum home on a large farm in 1840. Dr. Baker was mur-

Abner Baker

dered by Union troops in 1863, and the most reliable account of his death appeared in the Knoxville Daily Register.

The story reports that Dr. Baker, who was rumored to be sympathetic to the Confederate cause, was confronted in his yard by a Union soldier who threatened him with a gun. Baker went into the house and locked the doors, but it was soon surrounded by troops, who demanded that the men of the house surrender.

> "Mrs. Baker told the soldiers repeatedly that her husband was the only man in the house, and he would surrender if they stopped firing. But the soldiers continued to shoot through windows."

Mrs. Baker told the soldiers repeatedly that her husband was the only man in the house, and he would surrender if they stopped firing. But the soldiers continued to shoot through windows, and eventually broke into the house and made their way up the stairs. Baker was shot and killed when he opened the door to confront the assailants.

But that wasn't the end of the bloodshed. Steve Cotham, historian and manager of the McClung Historical Collection, confirms the story that Abner Baker returned to town in 1864, possibly seeking revenge for his father's death. He killed a Union officer, thought to be a man named William Hall, near the Knox County courthouse. Later that day, he was forcibly removed from the jail and hanged by a mob.

The Baker-Peters house is now owned by Larry Tragresser, who runs a dental practice out of the first floor. A door in his office with two holes is supposedly the same door Union troops shot through when they confronted Dr. Baker.

Some of the customers at Baker Peters restaurant, which occupies the second floor, think that Abner's unsettled spirit has never left the old house. Events coordinator David Poe says most employees, as well as a number of customers, have had strange experiences in the restaurant.

Eric and Johnna Dangle recall a time when they were sitting at the bar in the early evening with two other customers when Eric happened to look up at the exact moment two wine glasses shot off a rack above the bar and smashed into the wall. No one, including the bartender, was near the glasses, he says.

There are several pendant light fixtures in the restaurant, and occasionally one will swing. Some attribute the movement to nearby air vents. But all of the fixtures are near vents, and only one moves. Strange events are common enough that restaurant regulars no longer try to explain them.

"Everybody just looks at each other and says, 'Abner'," Eric Dangle says.

Robert Smith says similar phenomena occurred when the building was home to the Hawkeye's II in the 1980s. He recalls hearing loud, unexplained sounds coming from the attic. Customers also reportedly getting locked in a bathroom that, at the same time, had no lock on the door.

"Do things happen every night? No. But I've seen things I cannot explain. It doesn't really scare me – it intrigues me."

Smith plans to be in attendance at a séance that will be held in the restaurant at midnight on October 31. Medium Steve Bishop will conduct the event. Poe says anyone can attend, but Bishop reserves the right to exclude anyone he deems disrespectful.

While he appreciates the publicity the restaurant receives from having a resident ghost, Poe says it's a double-edged sword.

"I'd rather be known for our great steaks than our ghost."

CHAPTER TWENTY

A Spirit Lives On
at Greene's Antiques

Every home has a story

The original stuffed Santa stayed in the dormer window above the front door for years until he became to sun damaged and fragile. A new Santa took its place and remains there year round in Sarah's honor.

Tonni Sledge
Savannah Courier

A beautiful old home sits on Wayne Road in Savannah re-minding passers-by of the grandeur of days of yore.Every home has its story. This home, however, seems to have its story still existing within its walls.

The home of Sarah McAnally, now Greene's Fine An-tiques and Interior Designs, is a place of beauty – and curi-osities.According to its employees, Sarah McAnally is still very much a part of what goes in her former home.

Millie Greene purchased the home after her store on Main Street in Savannah burned around two decades ago. From the time she began moving in, she and her employees realized some-thing different was going on there.

"You can feel her presence still in the house. Something happens and you just know – it's Miss Sarah," said Greene with a smile.

When Sarah McAnally built the home, it was state-of-the-art. It was her passion and she went at the project with gusto.Her husband, R.H. McA-nally aka "Mack," drowned in a farming accident just as construction was beginning. Sarah supervised the con-struction closely.

"The home was built by Douglas Blount. He passed away last year, but rumor has it that if she had a question, she'd knock on his door at home no matter the hour," said Greene. "I was even told she'd go sit on the bed in his bedroom to discuss the house. I don't know that it's true, but that's been told me."

The house has been renovated to accommodate the store, but for the most part, Greene has kept the home as true to its original design as possible. The kitchen appliances are all original and working except for a dishwasher that was re-placed by a prior owner.

Sarah McAnally, 36, as niece Judy Flanagan remembers her; regal stately and beautiful.

"I have been told that she would invite the home economics students over from the high school to use her kitchen," said Greene.

Judy Flanagan, Sarah's niece, remembers the construction and walking over paint cans when she was 4 years old. "If anybody wanted to go out to eat she'd tell them they could, but she preferred to eat at home," said Flanagan. "She would always say

This photo was taken upon arrival at Greene's Antiques. The door was ajar, but the broken pieces were on the outside side of the door.

she'd rather be home than anywhere else."

Greene says strange hap-penings are common in the home, though. It's not unusual to arrive in the morning to find every light on throughout the house – including the closets.

On one occasion there was a shattered shelf lying next to a three-tier glass stand. The design of the rack made it im-possible for the shelf to have dislodged and fallen on its own.Summer Moore is an em-ployee of Greene's Fine An-tiques. She told of an occasion when she and a co-worker were in the back portion of the house.

The doorbell sounded so they checked the video monitor. They saw an older lady with a bun bending over in what was formerly the living room.Walking to the front to assist the cus-tomer, she found no one. Continuing throughout the building, she never found a customer. The doorbell had not sounded again to signal an exit.Sue Smith, also an employee of Greene's, is com-fortable with Sarah's presence.

"I'll come in a room and there's a purse or jewelry on the floor. Or we can hear jewelry tinkling, but there's no wind in here," said Smith."But she's a good spirit. She knows we're tak-ing care of her house."

Those who are in the home regularly are convinced Sarah is with them as well.

"There is a hanging light fix-ture in the kitchen. A couple of us were working in there when it began to swing," said Greene."No fans were on, no win-dows open, it just started swinging."

A notable event occurred not long ago with another glass shelf, this one an enclosed cabinet. Greene arrived one morning to find collectibles shattered outside the door of the cabinet.

"The door was slightly ajar, but the broken items were on the outside of the door. The door should have been wide open because of where the items were," explained Greene. "I still can't explain how they got out of the cabinet and on the other side of that door."

The original Thermador ovens installed when the house was built are still working today.

While Sarah lived, she kept a stuffed Santa Claus in the dormer window above the front doors. The original Santa became too fragile and now re-sides with Flanagan, but a new Santa remains in the dormer window in Sarah's honor.Sarah passed away at her home in 1994 with family close by.

"She was one of the great ladies in my life," said Flanagan."I liken her to Barbara Stan-wyck's character in "The Big Valley. The way she carried herself – she was the matriarch of our family. I even recognized some of her furniture on the show, it was exactly the same."

Are any of the staff at Greene's Fine Antiques troubled by the strange goings on?

Not at all. When something odd happens, they often say, "It's just Sarah."

Ghostly PLACES

Crossword Puzzle

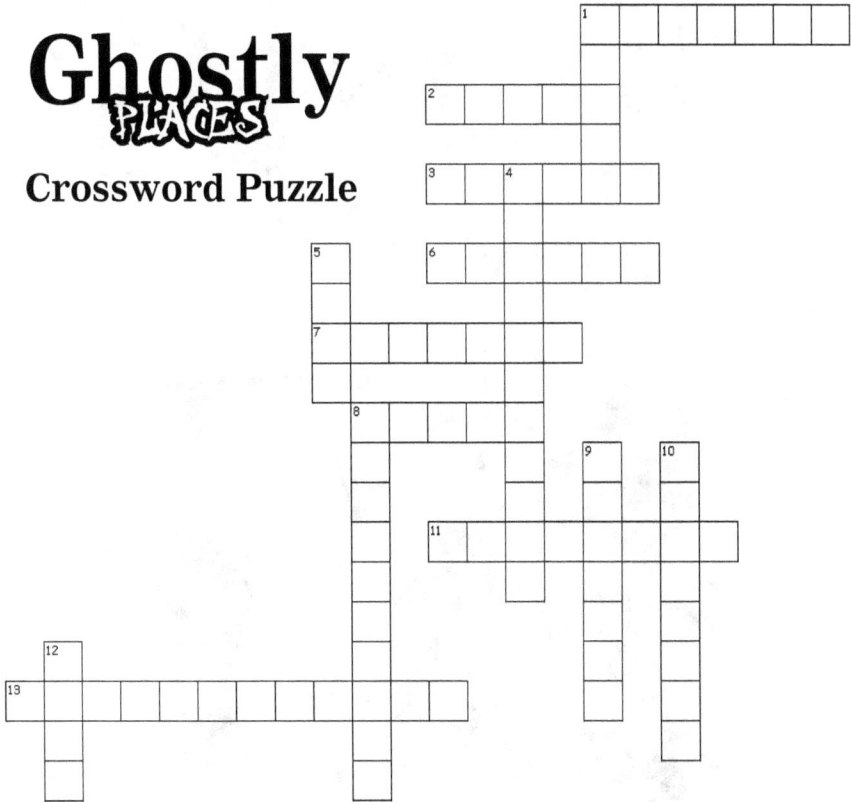

Across

1. Haynes body found near this window
2. Color of Captain Clay's horse
3. After dash in Baker home
6. Last name of grave digger
7. She was found dead in the Haynes home
8. Last name of Knoxville paranormal historian
11. House name on page 38
13. This Tennessee town has a ghost-finding business named "Ghost Busters"

Down

1. Name of doctor killed by Yankees
4. Historical Macon County landmark
5. The witch in the Clarksville area
8. Haunted tunnel
9. Type of rod used to find an object
10. This type of spirit was found in Canton
12. Location of downtown prankster

Ghostly PLACES

Brought to you by the 125 newspapers who make up
Tennessee Press Association and Tennessee Press Service

www.ingramcontent.com/pod-product-compliance
Lightning Source LLC
Chambersburg PA
CBHW052217270326
41931CB00011B/2386